Polarization
in America

it may be winning,
*but it's **not** working!*

JOE COUCH, MBA

ISBN: 1463742606

ISBN-13: 978-1463742607

Joe Couch

**This book is dedicated
to
the future of America**

CONTENTS

BUT I BELIEVED YOU!

- They told me if I got an MBA from a top school, my success would be virtually assured. I believed them.

- They told me if I went to an Ivy, my life would be enriched and that I should not worry about taking out student loans. I believed them.

- They told me if only I started a business for myself, I would be my own boss. I believed them.

- They told me if only I got a government job with a defined benefit pension, my retirement income would be certain. I believed them.

- They told me if I followed my executive contract and filed a report to help protect a woman when she complained about harassment that I would be protected from retaliation. I believed them.

- They told me if I gave my time to social causes that I would be surrounded by people with ethics and morals. I believed them.

- They told me if someone gave deposition testimony, they would tell the truth. I believed them.

- They told me "*the* (big) *money will come*". I believed them.

As of today, **they all lied in one way or another**.

You are welcome to think that it was just my naiveté operating at each step, and maybe that they lied should not matter in and of itself, but the problem for you, your children, and your grandchildren is that *they do not care* that they lied, distorted, misrepresented, or out and out covered their butts, legally or illegally.

What did I learn? While I had suspected it for some time, these experiences confirmed for me that this country is suffering under the disease of apathy through *voids in character*. In other words, we have a huge and growing void where character should exist.

It is a poisonous assault on our civilization and the American Dream *from within*: one unethical person sliding down the slippery slope at a time, supported by other unethical people turning the other way or doing nothing even when legally required to take action. In aggregate, this erosion has had large social, economic, and political impacts.

Simply said, I believe America is destroying itself because we accept apathy and dishonesty from one another as the coin of the realm: by allowing *a little bit* of lying or cheating or distorting as an acceptable part of our daily transactions; by breathing in and out the phrase *"so what?!"* and *"what's in it for me?"*.

It's my reasoned opinion, after seeing a lot of really outrageous things happen, in politics and work environments, that many people rationalize behaving badly as fully justifiable in terms of reaching the American Dream. They lack worry about their own unethical or gray-area behavior if their lives remain unaffected as a result of the way their decisions impact others.

While this book is intended for everyone, I hope a good number of managers, college students, and people in the middle-upper class, take time to hear me out. If we are to seek change or *be the change*, it's my contention that one of the fastest ways to do so is to request of those who have or likely will have some economic and political power to reconsider how they operate.

How managers and high net worth people treat those "under them" is highly impactful, because their behaviors and decisions both ripple through the organizations they run and the causes they support, and influence the people who admire them. College graduates are the managers and middle-upper class people of tomorrow, and to the extent that this book says a lot about the future, it is hit right up their middle.

However, this is not a book intended to trash the people in charge or beat up on one political side more than the other. To be clear, *I do go after the*

political parties strongly here, but it's in the context that their polarization is the problem; finding ways to reach compromise is the solution. In sum, I ask you to consider that it is our task as Americans to admit that no one political position alone can solve our challenges, and instead, that we seek a problem solving orientation, for I believe that doing so might just be the only way out of the mess we are in.

I think I've seen just about all the hypocrisy possible, but I *promise* you this is not a book that whines about my life. Somehow, in spite of it all, I am still optimistic about America's future.

I believe we need to adopt a different way of thinking and behaving that many Americans do not currently embrace. It is an integrated thought process that asks you to tie together the disparate problems we face and shows how our individual tolerance of bad behavior has amassed into the overwhelming problems that we as a country face going forward.

That said, as I make the case for this change to you, I have to say that I am not an investigative reporter or an academic. I will tell you where I got story data, but I generally do not spend a lot of space telling you what the precise page of the NY Times or the Wall Street Journal it was on, particularly if I first read it online, i.e. there may not be a way to know what on-line "page" it was on.

Finally, I am not that unique, just verbose with examples to share. If you got something from what I have to say, the best way to return the favor is if you talk with others about the arguments I pose here and become a part of the solution.

Go USA!

"WHERE THE HECK IS MY BREAD!?"

Right now, most Americans are in denial about our interdependency. Let's take a simple example.

Generally, many do not highly value the high school educated, yet safety trained, truck driver who brings the bread to Safeway or Wal-Mart. Somehow, magically, that loaf just gets there and dang it if they do not have your favorite brand in stock. And so we stand there in front of the bread rack, thinking:

*"Where the **heck** is my bread!?"*

This is the (sanitized) first thought that goes through many people's minds. Yep, in denial or at least, in deep forgetfulness about the real interdependency that is required to make a loaf of bread and get it to market. Most people do not often have the knee-jerk thought that some external reason could be the reason why the loaf was not there, even if the facts simply could be that the grocery store was sold out.

What if the truck driver had been in an accident and was critically injured? Unless facts of the accident are brought to our attention right away, we often assume some *intentional* force was behind the missing loaf and initially react with a sense of being denied; after all, we deserve choice - all the time - every day.

This thinking pattern repeats in other areas of life, and now, it seems to me, our society is has become somewhat dysfunctional, with many people having become convinced that personal desires can be directly converted into reasonable expectations about *how things will be*, now and in the future. *After all, the Jones have a big house, two cars, month long vacations in France, so it can of course be mine too.* In other words, I believe high - and perhaps excessively high - levels of expected entitlements, conjoined to the concept of the American Dream, have been broadly accepted in this country, across **all** socio-economic spectrums.

While some are interested in these ideas of how things *should or will be*, I find myself more and more interested both in observations about *how things are* and in examining the contradictions when things differ from what people feel ought to have happened or differ from the way we feel things should happen in the future. The issues most likely will not be new problems to you, and I do think being somewhat humorous or highlighting the irony through example can help the dialogue more than simply offering a critique, and so I do both.

I vote on both sides of the aisle, so I have no one particular ideology to put forth except perhaps "avoidance of doing the same dumb thing over again and expecting different results". I believe you'll find that I examine bad behavior without much prejudice: both sides get doused here.

Why I am writing this book is that I have found myself in discussions with people about life in America and they have said things like, "*You should be a radio talk show host*". I'm not interested in doing that, but these issues bother me enough and I have come to know that there is a dialogue that people want to have in order to push life further in the direction of solutions.

One of the problems, from my perspective, is that most Americans have not been taught to interpret information with the goal of understanding how various areas of life fit together from *an integrated view*. It is not our fault; we are not fundamentally deficient; there are just a lot of reasons why the average citizen is not induced or trained to take a hard look at the problems we face from a non-polarized approach. **This book brings together ideas that may seem like they don't go together, but my contention is that they do go together, if only that they impact each other and if only that they belong together in a more complete American dialogue**.

One deterrent force to our learning integrated thinking is that some people, often those in powerful positions, economically benefit if they can keep the state of affairs in an oppositional state, fueled by the use of simple polarizing slogans, and it seems to me that they actively work to keep things from actually being solved.

But I just don't think it is working for us anymore to look at problems in a standalone fashion - it's all inextricably linked; life both operates in a context and is a context itself. Our problems do not exist in a vacuum; they are woven into the social and value driven fabric we call America.

THE POWER OF MENTAL CONFLICT

We are going to avoid almost technical psychological terms, but studies of how people think, or "have cognition", have resulted in a powerful theory of motivation about why people do what they do. Psychology can be rather *whack-a-mole* in attempts to use scientific methods to predict human behavior, but one of the most effective explanations for why we do what we do has evolved from cognitive approaches, so much so that most psychotherapy has now shifted in this direction.

At core, why do we have so many problems that are stagnant in being addressed, let alone solved?

I contend that it's a lot about the power of *cognitive dissonance.*

Cognitive dissonance is a concept that specifically came from social psychology research but is one of the theories that us mere mortals can understand with some ease. This concept can help us look at American behavior more clearly and arrive at some answers as to why people have a hard time remaining loyal to even their own fundamental expectations about character.

From Wikipedia, *cognitive dissonance* is defined as "*... an uncomfortable feeling caused by holding conflicting ideas simultaneously. The theory of cognitive dissonance proposes that people have a motivational drive to reduce dissonance. They do this by changing their attitudes, beliefs, and actions. Dissonance is also reduced by justifying, blaming, and denying.*"

That defined, I'm not going to sit here and play amateur psychologist on every issue, but where the concept seems to help answer why people make decisions that illustrate voids in character, I am going there.

So, it's my contention that a lot of the "*so what?!*" or "*what's in it for me?*" attitude starts with what they do NOT teach in most schools about generally expected adult character traits. Of course, it's also true that attitudes are learned through internalizing beliefs polished at home. However, there are social, legal, economic, and political forces in this country, not necessarily consciously working together, but nevertheless, combinations of these forces have created a situation where even those of us who are born with good opportunities cannot help but see that the future is likely going to be a difficult one, *even for us.*

Again, we have hard social and economic decisions in front of us. I contend that we experience cognitive dissonance or outright denial about how best to solve those issues, because generally speaking, the least socially harmful or needed road may have moderate to large economic consequences for our own lives and that of our families.

We therefore many immediately deny they are *our* problems or we may go through a process to move significantly away from our prior, strongly held beliefs to another point of view that helps rationalize that those problems are *over there*. We neatly trick our minds into believing that we are safely insulated in us-ness: as in *this high status life belongs to us, not them, therefore, I will vote to sustain my lifestyle.*

It is my contention that rationalizing like this is **not** political party specific; it is a personal approach to life that, when in aggregate, has provided the motive force for the social and political polarization that we now experience.

As anyone who has been battered down a bit may already suspect, as we look to the future, warning signs are present that many may simply have to give up "living large" as an inherent American goal. The indicators are all around us and the media has even covered the issue, though perhaps not as directly as they should have.

In my opinion, for most of us, living more simply with less "footprint", may not be a choice. This idea however conflicts for most of us with the Declaration of Independence's statement of our right to the "*pursuit of happiness*" and so we are confronted with conflicting ideas about how to get there.

We often are faced daily with decisions, large and small, about how to *obtain more happiness.*

Generally, as peer pressure and advertisers tell us, that means the pursuit of a larger personal footprint: a bigger house with more electronics, a pool, a hot tub, a more prestigious car, and so forth. I have no moral judgment about whether or not a bigger personal footprint is a good thing to do in and of itself as I spent a lot of time seeking some of these things for myself, but I am faced with some inarguable facts.

One of the main observable reasons for the expected change in future lifestyle is that the earth's resources are limited. Other growing economies will simply not take *no* for answer in sharing those resources *and they are not,* China and India most notably. This pattern will, in the not too distant future, likely have noticeable economic impacts on the prices and availability of goods, which will in turn, probably impact our standard of living across the board.

So, what I personally expect to see happen, and there are signs of it already, is that at least some people *will start to adjust their viewpoint to avoid cognitive dissonance about the approaching change in quality of life.* They will perhaps tell themselves that living a simpler life is not "settling" for less, and instead will applaud one another for using innovative, green, or other solutions. This change will create a *new* peer pressure to reward those who respond nimbly and in advance to the forecast data in front of us.

That's the outcome scenario that retains a positive bent: *and they lived happily ever after with reduced expectations.* The negative outcome scenario is just more of the same to get "*what's in it for me*" - and that one seems more likely unless there is a change of heart at the level of the individual, perhaps all 300+ million of us.

So, what happens when there is less stuff available and a great number of people still think they all are entitled to a piece of it?

I shudder to consider what the worst possible outcome might be.

But for now, let's focus on seeking solutions and get on with our conversation.

THE MEDIA

The media is almost totally bought and paid for. It's been said many times before, but it's worth repeating because it underlies the rationale for this book, for if they told you how it is like I'm going to tell you how I see it, I would not have written this book. People with access to the media control the information we use to evaluate our world: the media influences the developing adolescent viewpoint in terms of what's cool or not and it impacts what we decide is relevant as adults, like the Rolling Stones.

So, keeping it real, on their own merit, would we be interested in 70+ year old people who play electric guitars? No, they get air time because they have a position in our history through media coverage and because people tend to respond positively to nostalgia. Take it from an MBA, the media and marketing folk know this. They know you want to remember when you had no wrinkles and far more hair, but they also know you like to see how old Mick looks so you can feel not so bad about yourself.

So beyond crisis coverage, it's a daily game for the media and marketers to fill up air and print space with news and human interest stories that they hope will attract your emotional buttons, in part so that you will watch the commercials. Maybe that would be fine if they actually told us a fair version of the news; but they also push a point of view so those ideas of yours which at least moderately align with *their* values are reinforced in *their* favor.

Is this bad, perhaps just *a little bit* of bad?

Well, what happened in America in media over the decades is that there were numerous mergers and acquisitions of independent stations, thus almost eliminating potentially nonaligned voices, leaving PBS, the BBC, and Reuters as probably the only ones as less than moderately partisan. My soapbox about broadcast news is petty - OR - *maybe it's not* and points to a dramatic shift in the country in terms of attitude.

You decide.

I admit it - when the newscasters tell you every four minutes, "*Coming Up Next*" and then they show all but 10% of the story, and hold the other 10% until the last viewing segment - the hair on my neck stands up. Do they really think we are that dumb or sedated?

The marketing technique to get me to stay until the end and watch all the commercials has almost totally by itself turned me off to TV news. Even as I write, I hear Anderson Cooper saying "*Coming up next....*" Look, buddy, I am watching the news, and I am going to watch however much of it I am going to watch. You can't trick me into staying any longer than I want to and you **ARE** getting me to switch channels if you push a teaser multiple times in 30 minutes.

Also, any story about the newscasters themselves drives me up the wall. *Who cares* about who is on the newscast? I do not. Just tell me the news! I don't care if they have stopped dyeing their hair. Somehow it was newsworthy to a station I happened to flip on during a business trip to do a full length story on why the woman anchor had stopped dyeing her hair. Not news. Not interesting. I say: Get the priorities straight! We have some problems in this country that stories about news anchor hair dye will <u>not</u> solve.

So, after about 10 years of this growing annoyance with broadcast media, I have come to rely about 90% of the time on the internet to read my daily news unless it is a major disaster. Half of what hits the airwaves these days seems to be from Youtube and Facebook anyway. In fact, the news conglomerates are responding to the trend and it seems that more and more often the stories now start out with, "So and so *blog* broke the story..."

MAKE WAY FOR THE BLOGS

What is interesting about all of this, especially when U.S. Representative Anthony Weiner in 2011 texted his body parts, is that the bloggers are getting some air time and they are *not backing down* to major media. They are saying, to paraphrase: *We told you! You ignored us! It was only because we showed a reporter naughty shots that you took it seriously!* In other words, the media failed to do its job unless embarrassed by a blog into doing it. But whew! What a relief that at least the media finally took Weiner's crotch *seriously.*

Ok, the point here is that we the public are taking the *blogs* <u>seriously</u> because we no longer trust the information coming from the conglomerate media to be unbiased. When one network calls itself "fair and balanced" and another has anchors who all almost scream monotonously about unfairness, it all sounds like one cacophonous rattle. They are so busy promoting their political slant that we end up, if we are not true believers to their cause, simply being distrustful.

For myself, I am now *highly* suspect about how often the media, *or anyone who seems to be using media methods,* is doing product placement when the story line tries to make referring to a specific product seem innocent. If a company owns both consumer products and TV networks, their products **are** making it into programming. *It's just where it's at,* you might say, but I do not have to support it by watching: I am voting with my feet and moving my attention span elsewhere.

Here's a good example of someone who is clearly using media methods: Eckhart Tolle (a guy with his own spiritual TV channel) had his staff posting his comments on Facebook. Recently they made a big hoo-hah about how much ET was *"enjoying his new iPad"* and how that would make it easy enough for him to do his own postings. Well, was that a product placement for the iPad or not? I personally could not tell, but I definitely could not rule it out either.

He went on to post something that many of his fans thought just could not have been from him, so much so that fans claimed *maybe a hacker* had somehow got on the official ET Facebook page and posted under his name - sound familiar? At least some of the 400,000+ fans on his facebook page could not be wrong, now could they?

Cognitive dissonance in action: the upset fans had two conflicting thoughts about Eckhart Tolle, so it's my opinion that some resolved the dissonance in these competing ideas by adjusting their belief such that the poster could not have been Eckhart Tolle and so their discomfort resolved. Tolle did not respond to the fan debate at all, and has proceeded to post more messages since then, thus clearly suggesting that, in fact, it was he who had posted the controversial message.

I should probably say that most fans never wondered about whether or not it was him. But the ones who questioned the identity of the poster did so harshly. They were argumentative and aggressively trying to get others to move towards their point of view.

So this may be a funny example to you, and maybe it's what you get sometimes when those self-proclaimed religious guys are not rehearsed; maybe his unedited self did not align with his polished self, but he's also the guy who claims he's spiritually enlightened and that he is One with his True Self. Well, whichever self he is, claiming enlightenment is a pretty big claim to never screw up on. Oh well, it was just *a little bit of bad.* For the average Tolle fan, it was not really important, and probably it is not, so he's off the hook and they will forget about it by tomorrow.

Me? I'm still wondering if the iPad was conscious product placement and what he may have received in return as compensation.

Now Tolle is not exactly front page news, still his situation explains media dissonance rather cogently, but what about important stories the media ignores that come back to haunt them, us, the country? And probably by now you are wondering, beyond what it sounds like and what you may intuit, just exactly what I mean by "*character void*"?

DEFINING CHARACTER

Not to pitch any particular definition of character, but I think it would be helpful to at least give one idea of how the definition of character can be framed - feel free to add or subtract a trait or two to suit your own purposes.

Wikipedia describes the concept of character as "*a variety of attributes including the existence or lack of virtues such as integrity, courage, fortitude, honesty, and loyalty...*".

In a nut shell, what I mean by *void in character* is that at least one or more of these core behavioral expectations are *lacking or totally nonexistent* in the person's behavior or in an event under discussion.

So, to give an example, former U.S. Representative Anthony Weiner's behavior illustrates just about exactly what I am talking about. He was hired as a *public servant,* into a role that requires public trust, and there we found him, boldfaced lying to CNN's Wolf Blitzer about how *maybe it was a hacker* who sent out sexually suggestive photos from his Twitter account. Boy, these hackers seem to get around in dissonance-land, don't they?

The problem that remains for you and me is that Mr. Weiner seemed to have *NO ethical problem* with distorting the truth. People on the Left in the media backed him, and backed him heavily, and instead pointed to uncontrollable genitalia wielding on the Right. Essentially the argument was that Mr. Weiner should stay on in this very important job *because* the other side got to! It started sounding like *"But Mom, Bobby's parents let him wreck **their** car last week!"*

What about the point of view that it was a man lacking sufficient character to remain in the job?

Finally, of course, it *was* viewed that way, after a 17 year old minor was found to have been involved with Mr. Weiner, even if, according to him, it was not "indecent". But, before that tidbit came out, it was apparently *indecent but okay* for him to stay on, according to Lefty pundits - and people wonder where our kids learn the attitudes and justifications for acting *just a little bit of bad.*

But please do not be confused: I am not defending the Right's sexual misbehavior. In my opinion, those guys should have been tossed out too.

And so let's talk more about *those politicians*.

POLITICS

Non-extremists usually think both parties are rigid and tend to dislike politics because they feel it's often ineffectual power grabbing. I find myself in that center most of the time, but we have to dive in here because it's a necessary part of developing an integrated view of what often look like unconnected trends and issues.

MOSTLY ABOUT THE LEFT,
NO REALLY, IT'S ABOUT BOTH

For this Joe, the Left looks fractionalized and dysfunctional. The generally accepted belief of the Left is that *diversity rules and class warfare must be undertaken to eliminate inequalities.* Well, if you can't get any consensus and keep nominating people who are extreme, and then lose seats because of special interests or dumb behavior, then it might be arguable to say that *diversity* can also destroy.

To say it another way:

I have observed many instances over the years by people on the Left where they make excuses for bad behavior by trying to persuade that the public should have "*tolerance of differences*", and that somehow it was a difference in culture or gender or race that was a justifiable explanation for why the person did x or y. They seem to believe that reference to social class or ethnicity can justifiably re-define bad behavior away from what a common sense view sees it to be: voids in character.

I thought that was going to be all I had to say on this topic, but then an example showed up that I cannot ignore. All I can say to preface is that I simply see no justifiable rationale for racism. You have no way to assess that about me, I know, but I can only ask you to take my word for it. It illustrates what I mean by embracing an apathy towards voids in character.

I flipped on the TV in late June, 2011, and happened upon a Tavis Smiley interview of biographer John Farrell, who has written a biography of Clarence Darrow. In conversation about Darrow's character foibles, Smiley brought up Martin Luther King, Jr., and referred to the understanding that while King did some great things for America, he was also a man with "*humanness*".

I took this to refer to the fact that it has come out in several places that he was quite the womanizer (for more, see the Wikipedia entry regarding interviews with King's own staff members as well as a CNN report of March 31, 2008 called "*FBI Tracked King's Every Move*"). But the womanizing was not the kicker. The shock to me in this interview was that Tavis Smiley referred to Dr. King and said:

"...*as...we learn more about King's humanness, for me that makes him even greater. That he was able to, in spite of those shortcomings... stay focused* (on the work)"

Now I cannot in good conscience assess Dr. King's character the same way as does Smiley. I understand the desire to feel proud of Dr. King, and there's a spot in my heart for the man. However, Smiley calls Dr. King his "hero" but then minimizes any potential cognitive dissonance he could have felt about that side of Dr. King by *denying the badness* of this behavior; in fact, he elevates it into "greater-ness".

In my opinion, Smiley went further than simply tolerating or accepting some deficit in character: he has **embraced and lionized** Dr. King's deficit in character. What an incredulous message to our young this publicly expressed view promotes.

Now, I am not going to turn this book into a litany of scandals, but, just in case you think I am here just to slam the Left, let's acknowledge that the key figure in the Iran-Contra affair, Oliver North, reached a similar level of blind hero-worship as well. There have been many occasions on which people publicly have hailed North as having great character and stated that what he did was just fine with them; heck he's even had his own TV show, and while North's convictions were vacated due to immunity, the facts are that he was initially convicted of three felonies. **Neither side has a monopoly on apathy towards voids in character.**

And back to the Left in general: from my viewpoint, you currently look simultaneously **disorganized and union driven** - an oxymoronic combination perhaps, but hey, there it is, and I perceive there to be loads of voids in character going on - at least as much as goes on in the Right. Further, those on the extreme Left, those who believe in just about every conspiracy under the sun, are seen by Joe and most of his other centrist friends as just not very bright, especially when they contend that 9/11 was faked and that it was an "inside job". Puh-lease!

So, to beat this drum a little further, the Left believes they fully understand all the motives of those on the Right; that by itself is arrogant. The Lefties I know think that those on the Right live in simply one or more, or even all of the following stereotypes: racists, homophobes, greedy Ayn Rand adherents, evangelicals, gun loving rednecks, or just flat out under-educated and socially unenlightened dumb-o's.

While some of those categories might be easy images for you to use to classify people you have met, it is obviously not the whole truth about the Right. The truth about most things is always far more complex, but that does not provide for teaser sound bites on TV news, so *hey let's ignore people as individuals and group them up. We can get more votes that way. We can get more viewers that way. We can build a coalition that way. Oh yes we can!*

See, here's the rub for a common sense person trying to find a philosophical home: there are plenty of Left leaning folks that I personally have seen talk Left-talk, but act in virtually ALL the ways that the Left claims the extreme Right does. Just take away that super liberal lawyer's Lexus and see what she starts screaming about in terms of others get, what she "deserves", and how she pays too much in taxes.

THAT UNDERGROUND SUCKING SOUND

The story I probably like the most along these lines was a well-paid, Left wing supervisor of mine, some decades ago, who thought it was fine to fraudulently bank $500 per month in taxable income by writing allowance checks to her son and then depositing them in their jointly named account such that the kid and the IRS never saw the money or the taxes.

Yes, I saw this happen; I even had the strange and curious opportunity to ask the kid if he ever got that kind of money from her: looking shocked, he said he never had. I realized that the boy probably did not even know what she did in the account, and I further wondered, since he seemed so clueless, if she had forged his name to open the account.

No, I won't tell you if I turned the person in, but the IRS website instructions for doing so are:

"... fill out Form 3949-A online, print it and mail it to Internal Revenue Service, Fresno, CA 93888. ... Although you are not required to identify yourself, it is helpful to do so. Your identity can be kept confidential."

According to the International Monetary Fund and the Washington Times (Dec 9, 2009), the non-tax paying or underground cash economy is estimated to be 13-15% of Gross Domestic Product in the United States and other highly developed countries.

If true, even at 13%, in 2010 that would have been an astronomical number:

$2,000,000,000,000.00

Just to get some sense of size, if this $2 trillion dollars were weighted average taxed at say, 20%, that would be another $400 billion in the Federal coffers. I do not think anyone can argue that we could use every penny of that $400 billion, and since it is an annual loss, I would contend that the underground economy is rather a large part of why we have so much government debt. Illegals aside (someone else's book), people with voids in character are **not** paying their share, but they **are** using public services.

My opinion: I am not into a lot of taxes myself and I acknowledge this is a little simplistic, but keeping it real, a *temporary* national sales tax of 0.5 - 1% on everything, including junk food and soda, for about 5 years would solve a heck of a lot of our problems, in part because the underground economy generally can't get around paying sales tax for large ticket items, at least not most of the time.

My point of view on taxes is that we pay far less in taxes than do those in other countries, and someone needs to pay for the roads and other services we need in order that we remain civilized, but when even the tax loving Left doesn't think it's a problem to not report income, and that supervisor of mine was not the only Left leaner like that whom I have known, then with what pure authority can they confront the Right on taxes?

I end up asking: Is the Left trying to force class parity just so they can "have enough" to fraudulently avoid paying taxes, rationalized by thinking "*the Right wing does this all the time*"?

No moral high ground is left on the Left when this sort of thing happens, and, from what I've seen personally, it's become common place for people along the whole political spectrum to raise the pro-verbial finger to the government.

FEAR! FEAR!

Speaking of morals and now bringing in religion to start illustrating some of the inter-relation that makes it all so complicated, as I write this chapter, the Mormon ex-governor from Utah, Jon Huntsman, who is kind of slippery to the Left, threw his hat into the ring for President. He does not do any crazy yelling, has his own money, and has a reasoned way of talking. I am not Mormon, but since he is, that will be used to scare people since no one bothers to read about Mormonism before they yell about it and think perhaps there is only one way people should deal with God. But hey, is that yelling much different than claiming Obama was born outside the U.S.?

Both are *scare tactics*; they are dumb scare tactics if you ask me, but if you got nothing else of substance to yammer on about, then it's no surprise that politicos resort to not so subtle "*posture the other as the enemy . . . it will create cognitive dissonance and folks will likely resolve those conflicting thoughts by taking one political side or the other. It doesn't matter if we lose a few because we'll firm up our base. Good thinking!"*

While many on the Right won't like the top two options for President being Mormons, what's more true as a factor in the General Election, in my opinion, is that just about any version of God really bothers a lot of people on the Left. Not surprising to me, at the end of June, 2011, a Gallup poll came out and said that Democrats are *more* opposed to voting for a Mormon for President than are Republicans.

In general, for the Lefties I know, *secular* change is what they want and many of them will tell you straight up: in their view, *people who believe in God can't be trusted to know what's good for America*. To me, it's a laughable point of view because it fails to be a defensible criterion to assess how other adults process information; as if believing in God meant someone were less intelligent.

This example should be sufficient to show why I can make this contention: Einstein strongly believed in a version of God acting behind the tick tock of the universe. Do you really think he was a stupid man? Not.

But this focus on the Right as being "intellectually unenlightened" creates an attitudinal discord that again focuses on *them versus us,* and I contend it permits rationalization for acts of *character void* by those on the Left in political environments. The projective view by the Left that the Right lacks depth or empathy is a result of *the same lack of meaningful processing about human behavior and motives* that the Left claims the Right is guilty of.

The Right has projective views of the Left too and I'll get to that shortly as there are people on both sides that count on the economic payoffs that come to them individually from political opposition being heavily in play.

Yes, there **are** those that take advantage of the sleight of hand that appealing to people's fear can do: sometimes these people are called *day traders,* other times they are called *eco-terrorists,* and at other times they are called *lobbyists*; clearly, at least to this Joe, they exist on all extremes of the economic-political spectrum.

RELIGIOUS RIGHTINESS

What's real, as far as I can tell from the people I know on the Right, is that the religious Right really do believe in the core idea of "*American Providence*". In other words, they believe God gave Americans this country for a Divine Purpose, that it is a promise to be realized, and that intelligent design is driving the ship. To show how historically ingrained the Providential view is, it was institutionalized in this country as "Manifest Destiny", a concept first articulated in 1845, which provided rationale for the push into the western states. Manifest Destiny emerged from the Papal Bulls, including the *Doctrine of Discovery* issued by Pope Alexander VI in the late 1400s.

While Manifest Destiny offered white America a lofty goal of Providence, it also, in part through the doctrines provided in the Papal Bulls, allowed people to rationalize the killing and enslavement of Native American and First Nation peoples under the theory that those people were non-believers. Fortunately, killing people using this justification is now illegal, but the conviction that it is valid to push Providential destiny persists, even in current politics.

As such, even if they run out of money, a lot of the Religious Right fully believe that the way to support God's plan for America is *to keep the money in the hands of those who are his servants so that God's future can be more rapidly arrived at.* If they are being honest in this perspective, from a logical analysis, it is a defensible position for their rest of their politics, as everything else they believe about taxes, social programs, defense budgets, healthcare, and so forth falls out from this personal conviction.

So, even if I personally think the Right is too restrictive in how they think our grouped money should be spent - and I do - the Constitution permits such a view of life and the partisans are sticking to it. However, if you understand the conviction of American Providence that underlies the Religious Right, you find that this understanding is contrary to the Left's simplistic interpretation that the sole motives of the Right are to "*keep people down*", maintain racial divisions, maintain an "each man for himself" orientation, and keep government small to allow everything but a "*Lord of the Flies*" scenario to manifest.

The Right does collaborate, more often with those that think like-mindedly, mainly because they have a shared view of life. It's my opinion that it is not the reverse: it is not a view of politics that defines what is important in their lives. It's not "wrong", and the Left have that same kind of motivation too, but it's just good to **make it conscious** that a lot of people's driving motives come *from their personal beliefs*, not from the sound bites of party politicians who generally push an economic or philosophical motive. Dismissing people on the basis, then, of "*Oh he's a Republican - don't bother reaching out*" does both sides a disservice in terms of developing the ability to mutually work together.

One good example about the misinterpretation of personal beliefs is the task undertaken by Mormons to keep a year's worth of food stocks. It's part of their religion, they do it in "cells" and it makes them automatically interdependent on other Mormons and therefore not interdependent with Baptists, for instance. It is not a statement about excluding other groups in and of itself; it is a behavior that is based on their choice of inclusiveness based on a religious belief.

Group behavior like this is part of the complex and interlocking fabric of how things happen in this country and it helps to be clear about that when assessing the motives of others. In other words, not everything is done solely from "*what's in it for me*" perspective. It's been my experience that it can be hard for Americans to tease this difference in motives apart, but I believe we need to do it more often in order to reduce the polarization that causes the government to bog down and at times freeze.

Unfortunately, personal choices to support an activity can be distorted by those interested in polarization to further distance their group from mutual understanding and compromise; they may find it pays to push the sound bite, if only to get themselves jobs in a national political action committee. It's our job to confront those sound bites and call them what they really are: *inflammatory sloganizing, grounded in an appeal to fear.*

BUYING THE UP AND DOWN

And having said all that, to leave you with at least one positive takeaway, what is clearly good about the Left's economic policies? More growth has clearly occurred under the Left than the Right (NY Times and Washington Post articles, August, 2008). The data shows this really without much contradiction, and if you know that, and now you do, you may find yourself voting more Democratic than Republican even though you have a business degree and believe strongly in free markets.

- OR -

You may intentionally vote one way in one election and another in the next to do your part to create ups and downs in the economy and in the stock market so that you can take advantage when other people bail out of the market in the downswing - to buy stocks on the cheap.

Hmmm, think anyone does that? Beyond the day traders, do you think big banks and corporations fund both political parties at the same time just to "gain access"?

What if there is another clever reason, or maybe it's billions of reasons, that are printed in green ink? Not accusing anyone in particular of doing this as a political strategy, but plenty of investing people have been quoted as saying something along the lines of "*who cares about politics or the direction of the Dow, we make money no matter what*".

Just suggesting that one might think differently about corporate political donations and how people might be motivated in their voting habits. Maybe they do want policies to change, but maybe it's not just in one direction; maybe it's in both.

MOSTLY ABOUT THE RIGHT,
NO REALLY, IT'S ABOUT BOTH

Now you might expect an MBA to get deep into the non-religious Right, one way or the other, and I do go deeply into the Right in the chapter on Emotional Manipulation, so it is coming. I had to decide where the line should be for this book, and because I want to look at polarization, I am looking mainly at the extremes of each side. Further, on certain social issues, it's been my experience that the Right-leaning corporate business community is center, offering domestic partner benefits and the like, so in some ways, they are a fish out of water for this conversation.

But in case you think I was too harsh on the Left, there are a bunch of commonalities that perhaps should concern Americans about those on the Right.

In my opinion, there are very close minded people on the Right who think that racism and sexism are justifiable in political office, but they generally are marginalized. It does not take much to get them off the stage politically - give them enough rope and they generally do it to themselves - to wit, David Duke and the Ku Klux Klan.

Some will disagree with me about my position on privacy here, but bear with me if you do not agree, because my point for this section is *to highlight the extremely divisive things that are preventing us from solving problems.* Eventually, we'll need to leave at least some of them at the door to reach solutions, but first, we have to understand one another better.

One problem that confronts an America that needs to learn to compromise is the Religious Right trying to impress their idea of "Providence-appropriate" beliefs and behaviors on others, e.g. "*if you don't believe in Jesus Christ as He is defined by us, you are unsaved*".

I do not care if they try to persuade people about their views of God during their private time, but if we're going to solve the problems facing America, it's probably going to go much faster if the Right does not try to push their ideas about private behavior into a policy issue.

My opinion: Some people believe imposing their religious ideas has something to do with enforcing *good character* and so they feel it is justified to do so. They hate the sin, love the sinner, but dang it if they don't think you still should try to tell others how to behave or believe.

That said, I believe this conversation is where the definition of character must remain **separate** from any definition or opinion of what constitutes being obedient or devout in one's faith. The Founding Fathers thought so as well, which is why they separated church and state.

However, it's becoming clearer to me that we need to make the distinction between good character <u>and</u> obedience to one's faith a more conscious one if we are going to save America's future. In other words, one can have good character or behavioral traits and be an atheist; at the same time, one can have voids in character and still attend a place of worship. **Neither side of the religious aisle has a monopoly on character**.

So, because it is a big issue right now, I will plow right in: I personally think about the same-sex marriage debate in terms of it fundamentally being about the Religious not wanting the government to be able to tell them what to do, though I can't rule out that some of them also feel justified in pushing their definition of appropriate obedience to God on others.

However, as long as the government does not tell the churches what to do, it's my personal opinion that they all should make a deal: the Religious Right should stay out of people's privacy, and the state should stay out of any particular church's in-house rules. 53% of the U.S. population in a 2011 Gallup poll said they are now in favor of allowing same sex marriage. So am I - as long as it does not force a church to perform a ceremony.

Religions have a right to stick to the interpreted tenets of their faith, and by us allowing that, it means they will **never** have a right to tell you what you should believe or do in your church.

Free speech, separation of church and state, and all that: it's good stuff, let's keep it. It's more important than my personal opinion about homosexuality.

Another issue is that the Right *also* believes that they understand the motives of those on the Left. This is also arrogant, but it makes the two sides about equal in terms of arrogance. It's that groupiness that has led to more character void behavior - or in this case, justifying dirty politics to get what they want, and on the Right, Watergate and Iran-Contra are easy examples.

Here are a bunch of other opinions about the Right that are common stereotypes and help create unhelpful and persistent divides when exploited by the media and people in political office: The Right often portrays the Left as taking earnings belonging to the better skilled through the reallocation of wealth through taxes; the Right seeks to retain wealth for the few who already hold 1 - 5% of the wealth; the Right seeks to deny opportunities to everyone; and the Right believes in survival of the fittest and that *he with the most toys wins.*

I actually do not know how many of the opinions are dead on about either side. People vary widely in their beliefs; for example, some Libertarian Righties are fine with abortion and there are those on the Baptist Left who are not, and so forth.

My point: **stop the constant finger pointing.** We are almost all more complex and deep than a sound bite. Perhaps let's start acting like we know that. We might actually be able to solve some problems if we do.

BUT IT'S HOW THE POLITICOS *RESPOND* TO MONEY

Here's another opinion: the amount of money certain sectors have been able to accumulate is used to encourage hatred between the political sides. The Right blames Hollywood's liberals; the Left blames old white dudes at country clubs that still exclude women. In sum, and to a centrist, these blaming activities pretty much just cancel each other out.

But - they do create a constant noise - like an annoying fly.

It's my take that solutions can only be arrived at if we stop blaming the people with the money *per se* and start looking at the politicos who prevent tax money from being reinvested in truly *effective* jobs programs, for instance. Instead, funds or tax breaks are given to things that are not really economically helpful to create <u>significant</u> improvements in the economy, like corporate jet tax breaks.

Look, I'm not the only one who thinks there's a problem; most of *you* think so too. Recently, CBS started a series called "*Alienated Nation*", and they surfaced some eye-opening results about current American beliefs. Here are some of their findings:

- 69% said people like them "have little say" in what government does

- 80% said most members of Congress are mainly interested in serving special interests

- 66%, including 44% of Republicans, said "the rich benefit most from governmental policies"

- 71% think that special interest groups and 75% think that large corporations have "too much influence on American life"

So, we feel disenfranchised from our government and still we re-elect the same people and do not require them to make structural changes in procedures or decision making that would allow for breakthrough change to occur. That's our fault. We are responsible. We need to fix that.

Now, many people are really suffering in this country and we have a lot to do in terms of job creation, but we also need to keep it real in terms of how people with money are becoming an easy target for blame. A lot of them did not live large, a lot of them worked hard. A lot of them just were able, for one reason or another, even dumb luck or circumstance of birth, to have more money than average. A lot of them did not get there through voids in character (though it does not mean their ancestors were clean), but a lot of them have not done much of anything to hurt others in order to get theirs - and those are the facts.

And, if you've travelled around the rest of the world you would find that even the working class here is doing quite well as compared with their counterparts in South America, Africa, and Asia. I contend to you it is in part a matter of attitude: it's *just in our minds* that we think everyone ought to try to keep up with the Kardashians.

In other words, Americans often think that what they *want* is what they actually *need* - but that is not the global view.

Food, shelter, clothing and healthcare are still the *needs* you learned about in elementary school; and I would add that having a job and transportation also fall into the *need* category, as they are needed in order to obtain food, shelter, clothing and often healthcare. Everything else, if we're being totally honest here, is based on desire - on what we *want.*

Though I believe there will be more class parity in future years due to some complex reasons that are outside the scope of this book, what is true is that *it is just in our minds that it will ever be possible for everyone to have everything they want if only the policies of the government were different.*

Even if we solve a lot of the big problems, economic differences will persist in the world. It is just the nature of life that one person's talents and abilities are more financially rewarded than another's. The challenge is that we have to *stop emotionally discounting our own inherent worth* should we not be making $200,000 a year.

Why? In part, because you'll feel better if you stop beating yourself up about where you stand but second, because **the politicos use your emotional self-discounting to help maintain polarization in this country** - and again, that's getting us nowhere.

SO, *WHO* GOT THE MONEY?

The one nagging thing for me about the Right is that they do seem to get caught more often engaged in fraud and other white collar crimes and do not seem to receive adequate prison sentences proportionate to the potential long term harm caused. That is something that I believe smacks of an inequality the Founding Fathers did not adequately foresee or address. It also gives the message that certain kinds of void in character are almost okay, or at least minimally bad.

And - - the housing "*slam, bam, thank you ma'am*" rip off done by capitalistic banks, real estate agents, and mortgage brokers will likely impact *several generations in tens of millions of American families*. Clearly this was no small event; it seems to me that people with voids in character saw their opportunity to excessively satisfy personal desires and took it.

But a two TRILLION in meltdown followed by a return to the same old Wall Street bonus system that is still making a few capitalists crazy rich is rather revolting. It's really just unconscionable that they went back to the same games and that no law with teeth has been enacted to prevent the reoccurrence of maximizing bonuses at the expense of customers and the rest of the world.

If we had passed a law on it, maybe, as former GE CEO Jack Welch contended in a Piers Morgan interview, some of those folks would have gone to Europe or Asia to get the same pay packages, but I contend that there are plenty of folks who'd be happy to take those jobs without the extreme bonus packages. Some people might even think about those who leave: good riddance.

My opinion: *if this country is to fully recover, we have to be able to trust our leaders, not just in politics, but also in business.*

Fortunately, I say ironically, I was being beat up elsewhere and so was not involved in this particular debacle, but I watched with some horror from the sidelines. I did suggest to several people at the time that it was not wise to buy a house and that wages did not justify the prices, but only about half of them listened.

But this was *not* just a Right wing debacle and I will highlight at least one fact the Left probably does not want you to know, as it creates cognitive dissonance between this fact and the marketing message that *they* are the only political party with sufficient economic morality.

As Businessweek reported on February 27, 2008, Bill Clinton's "*The National Homeownership Strategy: Partners in the American Dream*" plan promoted - to the mortgage industry - that they should adopt "creative" measures to promote homeownership for those with insufficient income, including pushing for alternatives to a traditional model of down payment and market rates of interest, i.e. the birth of the low-doc mortgage started as a Lefty invention.

So, as we look back, we can see that <u>it took a village to create a meltdown</u>. It's not too late to get educated about what happened in the financial system, and as Americans who have hard decisions ahead of us, I believe we will need to get our heads better around what the mortgage and banking bonus-seekers did to our economy so we can take steps to prevent it from happening again.

While it's been framed as a Right wing issue, the fact both that Clinton pushed for "creativity" led the way to the low-doc mortgage and that a good number on Wall Street are in fact Left of center for their politics shows to me that the situation was really about "*what's in it for me?*" Yep, I contend that it was about some who were willing to push aside someone else's American Dream *at any cost* to gain their own.

There might be nothing wrong with a money focus in terms of morality. I can't judge whether it is or is not, but money's not something I have ever been solely driven by. **It's when going for the money is used as complete justification for unethical or illegal character-challenged behavior that I have a problem with it** and is when I believe we *all* should have a problem with it.

The American Dream has suffered as a result of these and other repeatedly unpunished, ill-prevented activities. Play above board and fair: no problem. Be underhanded and make illegal trades or allocations of stock into high net worth client accounts so they receive higher returns than the Joes of Main Street America: that I have a problem with. More could be done.

But the main take away I want to make here in terms of politics is that those who have most of the wealth and that people with money want to keep it - that's only natural on the surface of it. While it is not fair to blame the wealthy for everything, which was my prior point, wealthy people also know that it literally pays dividends to use that money to get what they want through the political machine.

The result of a motivation to keep what they have has contributed to increasing political polarization. I have to admit, however, that people's strongly held motives to maintain their wealth may make any change that the natural and economic environment may require of America very hard to accomplish without one or more major crises that impact the people with high amounts of wealth. In other words, we may find that it is only crises of high impact that bring those folks to their proverbial knees.

I contend that logic on its own is not likely going to be effective unless these people see enough good reasons to *choose* to change their views about how they operate in the world. I am not sure if policy or tax code changes can do it alone. This is NOT a call to arms or to terrorism; natural disasters may be adequate, perhaps one person's summer home at a time. However, the world has shown that if logic does not win out, then experience can do the trick. I believe some fallout from 9/11 proved that.

A New York Times survey, referred to in a September 7, 2004 article called "*A Universe of Loss and Recovery For 9/11 Families*", showed that 20% surveyed attended services more often after the 9/11 tragedy. I might have been happier if the survey had asked people if they themselves made a commitment to better personal behavior as a result of 9/11, but nonetheless I find the self-reflection and change in behavior that did result interesting, and perhaps promising.

To close, should you be interested in learning more about the banking crisis, there were some excellent Frontline episodes in 2009 called "*Ten Trillion and Counting*", "*Breaking the Bank*", "*Inside the Meltdown*" and "*The Warning*" should probably be on your to watch list. Also, the debacle is covered in several other books; ones you might check out include: "*The Wall Street Money Machine*", "*The Two Trillion Dollar Meltdown*", "*Too Big To Fail*", "*Fool's Gold*", "*In Fed We Trust*", and "*Chain of Blame*".

"I ASKED . . . WHO GOT THE MONEY?"

So, many believe, as the recent "*Alienated Nation*" CBS survey showed, that one reason for the conflict between the political parties is that they are too infested, in part by the wealthy, in part by corporate or other special interests. Inherent in this broadly held belief is an assumption that it's now **all about the money**. We have several nonprofit organizations now at work watchdogging the money and political influence, including the Sunlight Foundation, but are they enough?

Many people I know believe that all the politicos now do is just trade political favors: *you give me this, I'll give you that*. My guess is that a lot of people are not taught in their childhoods about doing things "for the principle of the thing" anymore. I certainly can say that most neighbor kids I knew growing up were not taught "for the principle of the thing".

As a result, I believe that politicians have now carried *highly refined* void of character behaviors into the government and that we are now witnessing the result of this developmental change in how people were raised in the late 50s through the 80s. The prior generation that Tom Brokaw wrote about in "*The Greatest Generation*" arguably lived more by principle than how people live today - what was good for the country was seen as good for them too.

But politicians have always struggled with the notion of *the public good*, and historically there have been times when significant change came about only when the imbalance became intolerable; Boss Tweed and Tammany Hall come to mind. However, I would contend that there is now little or no emotional conflict for the average politician these days, and that she or he often simply no longer struggle much with their conscience.

I contend that they do not live by the principle of "*what's best for the public good*"; they instead live by the principle of "*what's in it for me?*" lightly wrapped inside the words "*what's in it for my constituents?*" Now, it's not Boss Tweed anymore, or even Boss Hogg; it's simply "*I'm the boss*".

And courtesy of Mr. Weiner, we now have a nation perhaps starting to come to grips with the idea that women politicians may just have to kick a good number of the men out for doing the most dumb-o "*what's in it for me*" activity: not keeping it zipped.

Many people, including me, are starting to realize that women really do seek office "*to get something done*", (CNN, June 2011, Dr. Drew Pinsky). Men on the other hand, the research says, seek office "*to be somebody*" or perhaps, and this is just me talking, gain access to power in order "*to do*" somebody, or maybe several very much younger somebodies. But I digress towards potty-talk...

So we seem to have a pattern about sex and male politicians that is unfortunate - we probably have to admit that there is a trend here that is hurting our government - and so I have concluded that it is incumbent upon local voters, when starting to elevate someone up the public chain of command, to at least *not* vote in someone with a reputation for sleeping around. Just ask yourselves: do you want your grandkids to believe that *you* think these are the type of people who should be running the government? I don't.

It seems obvious, but maybe we should start voting for more mature people, not the "*maverick type who slaps me on the back, tells me he's my guy, smiles gratefully when he takes my check, and I get to convincing myself that little old one of him can persuade all those old wheeze bags into really getting something done - after all he's attractive, successful, and was my QB in high school - he'll get us a **win***".

Really man, who cares if your rep is female? She's at least motivated to do get something done, not simply there to elevate her ego and notch her guitar. Is she articulate? Does she share your beliefs?

I've had female bosses. They were fairer than my male bosses, generally speaking, and I didn't have to talk baseball with them every day. Work got done. I think we need a change there in the DC legislature in the personnel. I'm personally fatigued by thinking that a bunch of testosterone gets it done.

If this is a hard one to accept, just take a look at where letting things continue as they always have been got us. I could almost totally care less what party affiliation they have, I just think with more women we'd see a return to negotiation, of solving problems, not just the trading of favors, earmarks, and phone numbers for high priced call girls.

PORKY FRIED EARMARKS

Speaking of earmarks, let's get rid of them. Who let them happen in the first place?

A lot of us see them as one of the biggest symptoms of character void in action. Senator Tom Coburn has called earmarks, "*the gateway drug to spending addiction in Washington*". Even if politicians are so callused that they do not experience any cognitive dissonance when confronted with the decision about how to allocate spending, using earmarks clearly allows them to rationalize increasing the debt onto our future generations. Also, earmarks allow the "*what's in it for me*" to go unabated but for some opposing effort from the other party to bring home the pork.

As global citizen and CNN commentator Fareed Zakaria stated recently (either on the Daily Show or an Anderson Cooper segment), Europeans trust their federal government to know what ought to be done on an infrastructure and economic basis. He pointed out that Germany is a good example: though they take a sizeable chunk of taxes, the government is highly involved in plowing grouped money into specific industries to maintain competitive position.

My opinion: *that requires a people to be able to trust the government to be trustworthy.*

In America, in part because we allow persuasion in the form of paid lobbying, and all the other influence buying through political contributions, how can anyone think that we can trust the stewards of the federal government - *no matter which party holds the reins* - to decide where to reinvest the way they do in Europe?

Even a Joe sitting on some other couch knows that the politicians are bought and paid for and it's legal to do so. In fact, in January 2010, the U.S. Supreme Court blocked a ban on limiting organized and corporate political spending, so we now have *unlimited*, and now legally protected, influence peddling through political donations by the segments with the most money.

But why did pork-fried earmarks come into being in the first place? No one paying enough attention is all I can come up with. Perhaps each party had just enough "fat and happy" executives that they took advantage of the situation with placations to the mere minions: *we're taking care of you, don't worry about how.*

The country did fine for about 200 years without earmarks. Ronald Reagan vetoed a bill containing 157 earmarks in a 1987 highway bill, so earmarks are relative newcomers to the game. And so I contend that one can conclude that Congress funded personally politically advantageous projects in their districts and ignored the data in front of them that asked for decisions *for the public good* - information that would have told them to better maintain and fund the aging infrastructure for instance: roads, bridges, tunnels, etc.

DUDE, THE BRIDGE JUST COLLAPSED

One of the biggest problems we face, as a result of not spending for the public good over the last 20-30 years, is infrastructure, with $14 billion estimated as the cost for Pennsylvania alone to repair its bridges, according to a 2008 PBS "*Blueprint America*" story.

Further, Transportation for America data shows that about 11.5% of the 69,223 bridges in the country are now classified as "*structurally deficient*". That is over 700 bridges, transporting millions of people daily. The collapse in Minnesota of an arterial highway bridge in 2007 could happen just about anywhere. Who is doing anything about it? As far as I can determine, not one elected representative is clearly championing this cause in Washington, D.C.

The last Federal Transportation Bill expired on September 30, 2009, so as of today, nowhere near enough of our grouped federal money goes to maintaining, repairing, or replacing the infrastructure.

I ask you: *how will your loaf of bread get to market without a safe road?*

With the extreme pressure on state and local budgets limited to maintaining basic services (and funding pensions) for the foreseeable future, the need for federal assistance seems all but inevitable. However, an Urbanland report suggests that the politicians in Washington do not believe it's a politically important use of funds. Funding may not even be on the table until 2012 (*"Federal Transportation Bill Uncertain"*, June 8, 2011).

At the same time, at least one iconic bridge has been **internationally outsourced**. Who even knew that was possible?

A June 25, 2011 NY Times article, *"Bridge Comes to San Francisco With a Made-in-China Label"*, detailed that the new SF Bay Area Bay Bridge was being built in China and shipped over for assembly by American workers. State officials claimed that they had saved hundreds of millions by doing so, using cost savings and China's steel fabrication leadership as rationales. Why is it cheaper? Because Chinese workers are little more than slave labor as compared with the salary requirements here, even if everyone here were paid minimum wage.

And while politicians continue to export jobs for short term gain, what Arnold the philandering Governator's decisions did was to further enable the Chinese steel industry to land several key lucrative steel projects around the world, ones for which American firms in earlier times would have had a fair shot. In a nut shell, our government is effectively buying on the cheap and now, it can be argued, exhibits little or no loyalty to the U.S. economy, at least in certain industries.

My business training says there are deep benefits to a commitment to international trade. International trade, for instance, clearly mitigates wars, for countries gain more from trade than they do from war. International trade generally has now made war into something engaged in based on beliefs and rights instead of why it used to be done: natural resource grabs and trade routes.

However, as a result of this activity, even medium-term, we may have no American company able to be an internationally competitive steel fabricator should a pattern of importing such large ticket steel goods continue.

NO, "ROI" DOES NOT MEAN "RETURN ON IDIOCY"

Ironically, the Times' Bay Bridge article goes on to say that had California applied for Federal funding to assist in the construction of the bridge, they probably would have had to buy from American manufacturers. It seems to me that the Federal funds might have been able to make up the cost between "made in USA" or "imported from China".

So I just have to ask, is there anyone in California's state government doing any long term "Return On Investment" (ROI) math about how they spend money or whether that gap was coverable by the Fed funds?

And look, I'm no lawyer and I'm no "constitutionalist" as far as I know, but I ask you: *is it not almost to the point of being able to bring a lawsuit that presents the claim that elected politicians are failing in their legal fiduciary duty (or oath of loyalty to the Constitution) when they implement decisions that arguably do significant and measurable harm to each citizen's right to the pursuit of happiness?*

Just asking. There are limits on what you can sue the government for, and a lot of those makes sense, but I think I know just enough case law to think that there might be some merit to this idea. It's definitely worth publicly debating about. I pose the legal question to ask you to ask: *Where is that line?*

I really can't think of a great reason that, given the size and context of that project, made importing the bridge 100% justifiable. I will have people who disagree here, but look, first, *the government* should not be using free market decision making all the time. When it is such a large and strategic project, it should consider other factors and other stakeholders - after all, California is not General Electric, it is a state government that is supposed to be serving the interests of its citizens.

Second, the ROI calculation government should be using is at least a 50 year investment period that should include the long term secondary tax revenues that come to the state 50 years down the line from a higher paid workforce. I am not sure that happened in this case. I suspect it did not and I wonder how lobbyists factored in.

Clearly, to the average Joe, importing the new SF Bay Bridge seems to be a case of exporting U.S. wealth when other cost attractive options were probably available. It was arguably not loyal or dutiful, if you think about it, but I can't help but think that, for someone out there, it was and is "*what's in it for me*".

So, why a Federal transportation funding bill makes sense:

- So OUR people won't die in structural failures of deficient bridges

- There will be job creation for the unemployed people of OUR country

- There will be support for OUR industries as they attempt to complete domestically and internationally

SO WHERE IS *OUR* MONEY GOING?

So, just to provide some comparative data, just what *does* the Federal Government spend money on? To paraphrase, here's part of a list posted on December 23, 2010 on EconomicCollapse.net. You might wish to visit their site to read some rather amusing expanded descriptions of these projects. They tell us that in 2010 alone, our government spent our grouped money on:

- Creation of a museum in which to place retired neon signs – $1.8 Million

- Creation of a Grateful Dead Band location to archive materials – $615,000

- To pay for poems to be posted in zoos across the country – $997,766

- For an Internet dating study – $239,100

- To study male prostitutes in Vietnam – $442,340

- For a zoo to create a video game – $609,160

- To teach South African men how to wash their privates – $823,200

- To build/replace 36 potties in a park – $1.49 Million

- To build a new pedestrian bridge just steps from another pedestrian bridge – $260,000

- To create a display for a local banjo player in a museum – $1.5 Million

- To pay for a city's bike signage when adequate signage already existed – $900,000

This is why people like me go **HUH? What the ....?**

And we claim to be absolutely flabbergasted about how that happens.

Well, it should be no surprise, and here is some personal observation on the Washington DC scene. On a visit a couple of years ago, I found out that it is possible for anyone to lunch in the Senate lunch room to get some of that excellent "Senate Fried Chicken", in particular. So this Joe Couch and traveling companion did just that - a couple times.

There was the fragrance of an old white boys club about the place, no doubt, and it was like a country club: "the help" was mostly people of color, serving sweet tea on command; there was the gourmet buffet with a rather large selection of succulently roasted meats, hand carved by a chef; the desserts - they were truly fabulous, as was the dinnerware and the white cotton tablecloths. Dignitaries were present and the Senate Majority leader was not more than ten feet away shoveling food on his plate and responding to ingratiating greetings in stride.

But you know, the lobbyists know exactly where that lunch room is too, and we saw plenty of 300lb good old boys chumming it up on a first name basis with the staff and senators present. Something about that lunch room really bothered me. It was not as though my companion and I were prevented equal access, but still the whole situation stank of just that: unequal access; unequal power; unequal dinner tabs feeding unequal white guys stuffed into shirts way too small, bound up with ties way too tight around their bulging necks.

Maybe it was the sense that these were Midwest Farm Bureau types seeking more ethanol subsidies that appear to clearly cost us more than they give in return *OR* maybe it was *them* who convinced the government to spend close to a million dollars for *zoo poetry*. (I actually have a penchant for poetry, but this was a ridiculous way to spend a million dollars when we have so many other problems staring us in the face.)

So, although we went to just about every location of government in DC, even watched debate from the box seats in the Senate Chamber, the Senate lunch room was the *only* situation where I felt a tangible sense of political power. It was a clear vantage point from which to see how people *game* Washington. I recommend visiting should you ever find yourself in town.

Lunch was only about $15 with drink included as I recall. Anywhere else it would have been $25 or so - that's what the government vendor discount gets you. For what it's worth, I think I would weigh 300lbs too if I ate there every day, so maybe they should open a gym down there for the after lunch crowd - it might only cost the taxpayers as much as, say, the $997,000 spent on zoo poetry.

WE'RE TEETERING, BUT IT'S NO BACKYARD SEESAW

No matter how you look at it, it seems the whole lobbyist - money - access situation is extremely problematic to a country that seriously is in need of *more* ethical behavior, not *less*. I think everyone I have talked to about these sorts of affairs have about the same intuition: things have to change. People seem to be in some agreement that the way things have been going does not feel "in balance", for lack of a better word.

So, why is it not obvious then to pass lobbying and campaign finance reform laws? Well, *it is obvious*, but the sheer vast sums of money that fill campaign coffers and the supposedly needed millions to run for office make this near impossible at the present time. Money by itself is not evil, but a people who allows their government to become bought and sold does not seem like a society that could last that way indefinitely... and this is where authors throw in that old mainstay: *even Rome fell.*

Keeping it real, the opposition between the political parties is probably not completely avoidable and maybe it's even helpful on some level if some moderate conflict helps get issues into better focus or some laws into clearer language.

Still, it's not hard to see that the approach to trade item for item in budget or legislative negotiations is not driven by "*Ask not what your country can do for you. Ask what you can do for your country*" as John

Kennedy asked - and there's the rub. Back then, Kennedy's call was seen as a *patriotic* stepping stone to a new future and yet, if a young politician were to stand up today and say the same thing, s/he'd be ridiculed and so they don't dare repeat it.

It's just a heck of a lot easier to blame the other side on a Sunday talk show than to say, no, **this problem belongs to all of us** and we're going to sacrifice together to fix it together in order to come into better balance.

NO JOHN-BOY, THAT'S A PIT

To those of us who will have to work our butts off to fix the problems, the character voids have left us a nation in major debt, sending not only profits to China and other countries in an unbalanced way, but also by sending the interest payments on the U.S. bonds they buy, as our money presses work 24/7 to keep up with increasing "the debt ceiling".

And here we have a good example of how they manipulate by slogan.

For me, "*Debt Ceiling*" is a mentally conflicting phrase: it would not surprise me if you felt the same sense of confusion as I did when I first heard it. Call me a little paranoid, but I think just maybe some clever person phrased it that way at least a little bit on purpose.

Why? Because "*Debt Ceiling*" is the kind of term that calls to mind the hocus pocus of marketing. Without my mind doing anything requiring effort, it brings forth an image of openness, of ... *home, home on the range ... O beautiful for spacious skies, for amber waves* of - - ok, I'll stop - but the term *debt ceiling* sounds *almost blue sky airy and patriotic* when in fact, it really is a term meaning "*increase the pit*".

It seems to this Joe that the actions of politicians to increase the debt pit, without a clearly achievable plan to pay it off in a reasonable amount of time, implies another lack of fiduciary loyalty to the long term viability of America. They want to make the pit bigger, more expansive, but, long-term, it may just be the death trap for a society that still tells itself that it is the leader of the free world. Free to do what? Make economically suicidal choices? Well, these days, maybe yep, probably so.

They probably do need to raise it at this point for several years, and they claim that there are all these complicated economic levers of money supply and interest rates and currency value and that if we move too far long one stratum without offsetting one thing with another, we will have a disaster. But, clearly, us letting them continue to solve it with the standard economic modeling **assumes you believe that they know what they are doing**.

If you trust them at the Federal Reserve, for instance, then that entrustment lets the politicos trade for favors again, because they know this game of money supply and interest rates and how if they give in here, they can get something in return. See, fact is: they get paid no matter what it is they pass as a law, so, they rationalize, why not *game* something for themselves.

But "***Black Swan***" theory, brought forth by Nassim Nicholas Taleb, and lauded widely as alternative view to how economic events can occur, suggests that significantly impactful events happen irregularly by surprise and that we use hindsight to develop theories as to why they occur - BUT - at the time, before the event occurred, we ignored data that falls outside of our expected view that might have informed our actions differently (see Wikipedia).

So why don't we do more of that: question more of the current data, not just the historic data patterns that lead to some of the more popular ideas? Maybe we would come up with other economic inter-ventions - so who or what is stopping us?

I think you know.

And you might not like the next part of this conversation - because you probably currently believe that you really believe what you think you believe about politics, but I may just have an explanation for what the politicians and their friends are doing that answers part of why it is so hard for us to get out of thinking the same old way about economic issues - and to get out of the divisiveness that fractures and allows for void of character tactics to perpetuate themselves in government decision-making.

They do it right under your nose and at minimum, with tacit approval. In fact, most of the time, if you are strongly politically aligned one side or the other, you may actually be helping the "same old, same old" persist in a way that gives them momentum and energy to push forward with the way it's always been, and they do it through *emotional man-ipulation*.

EMOTIONAL MANIPULATION

*"I am right - it is **you** who are screwed up!"*

*"We've **always** voted Left/Right in our family."*

Most people think that they really agree with their party's view of priorities and values, at least most of the time. Well maybe, but what if I told you that they hire loads of psychologists, marketing, and political consultants to figure out the type of bills and messages to get out there, not only to get your vote, but *to develop **long term** group consciousness in you, your children, and in your network of friends.*

So I am going to tell you that, because they do. They have often applied the marketing principles I learned in college and grad school to manipulate people's emotions and build voting blocks. I contend that it is a conscious effort on the part of some of them, and some of them at very high levels, to build their base by appealing to the basic emotions of fear and anger.

Before I go further, I want to say that I strongly believe in social programs, but let's be clear: many of the social programs enjoyed here and in Europe are out and out luxuries, and are not achievable in developing countries. In "first world" nations, they are touted, often by the Left, as "*human rights*". Personally, I believe a lot of countries, including ours, have been rich enough to justify spending money on optional programs, regardless of the philosophy used to justify that spending.

But we are not talking about human rights most of the time here in America anymore; the right to not be murdered by your government is a legal human right, not an optional social benefit. I am talking about programs, like zoo poetry, that might be fine to spend on *IF* we have the surplus money to spend in this fashion, so I suggest we instead re-classify them as **optional** and "*only when there is sufficient surplus*". And as of 2011, I think most agree that we in American have little or no surplus to support optional feel-good spending.

Further, as taxpayers, we have the right to insist that social programs prove they work, whether classified as needed or optional. So, as far as we are able, I believe we should ensure foster care, housing for the developmentally disabled, medical care for the poor, and that sort of thing. However, there is also a place for encouraging our children and our communities to become more generous with their time and personal money to those less fortunate - it's just smart long term thinking, if nothing else.

I further contend that just because the government should do some basic things well does not mean that they should try their hand at everything. There are those in this society who try to convince common sense thinkers like me that we are "*bad people*" just because we act like adults when the going gets tough and we revise our expectations downward to pay for the essentials first and foremost.

These folks often then polarize any such open dialogue with inflammatory sloganizing. They seem to refuse to see that there is another view which strongly suggests that by reasonably tightening the purse strings now, there actually might still be a civilized society later.

THE LEFT'S EFFORTS

I am going to provide one in depth example in this chapter about how each side may be going about emotional manipulation, mainly because one example should do the trick.

So, let's start with the Left. In my opinion, the Left promotes the funding of liberal heart wrenching services, knowing that Left leaning and a good number of centrist voters will likely not vote to overturn them based on their emotions towards social causes. They count on the tendency of inertia and they count on cognitive dissonance to be resolved by each voter, if persuaded well enough, particularly through guilt, to go in their favor.

Here's the best example I could find for the Left: There is an interesting situation brewing in California that a blog in Fullerton, California unearthed about an agency called "the Orange County Children and Families Commission", also known as the First 5 Commission because it's designed to serve children 0 to 5. This agency was created by a tobacco tax law, Proposition 10, whose passing has been credited to the money and influence of Rob Reiner, of Meathead TV fame. It's somewhat comically called "the Meathead Law".

Apparently, the First 5 Commission receives about $500 million in tax dollars each year, but after 10 years, they still cannot show any proof via evaluation research that they have made a positive impact in the lives of children there. However, they *have*, according to their own publications, apparently spent much of their money on the Latino population, and have been shown to have underspent on African Americans and others as a percent of the population. It's not rocket science to theorize that perhaps this is intentional as the Hispanic voting block is increasing rapidly.

FOLLOW THE TAXPAYER MONEY

So - are they intentionally using tax funds to build a Left-leaning voting block in California, starting at ages below 5?

You decide. Here's their "follow the money" story:

First, none of my research contradicts statements newspapers and commentators have made about the alleged unwise spending of this agency.

I was not able to find one occasion where the First 5 Commission officially disputed data points made by reporters or commentators. One Commissioner actually admitted *on record* that they have not been able to demonstrate improvements ("*Fresno Co. finds it hard to measure First 5's results*", Dec. 26, 2009, Fresno Bee).

So, according to newspaper reporters, internet blog discussions, one Grand Jury report, and this Joe's common sense analysis, the following situation seems to exist in sunny old CA:

1. "*Unlike every other government organization in California, the First 5 Commissions have an exemption from the conflict of interest laws.*" **HUH**? Well, that quote turned out to be right: it's a limited exemption, so they vote on *each other's* programs, but nonetheless, it is one that allows the Commissioners who serve on the board to receive *all of the funds* if so voted on by the same group of Commissioners.

   A little favor trading and self-dealing going on, do you think?

2. It's been surfaced that the person who apparently *wrote* the First 5 law now has herself a state employee quality pension plan as the lobbyist for said agency, paid for by the First 5 Commissions. **HUH**? Yep - a lobbyist who is 100% paid for by public money. Did you Californians know they would use the money this way? I bet you didn't.

   Sounding like a Wall Street back room conspiracy deal right out of the movies?

3. Finally, a good number of these same First 5 County Commissions have decided to *sue* the state. **HUH**? The Jerry Brown-run government *legally* voted to adjust the Meathead law to take $1 billion of the First 5 reserves to fund poor

kids medical coverage for the fiscal year 2012 (which would have been unfunded if they did not redirect the funds).

However, several of these local Commissions seem to have decided that it is *their right* to sue the state. Why? Well it seems that they perhaps now think it's actually *their* money and not that of the taxpayers.

As one commenter succinctly put it ("*First 5 San Diego Votes To Cut Funds From Kids' Health Care, Education*", California Healthline, May 10, 2011):

"This IS what happens when you write into a law that the foxes can guard and eat from the hen house - and the Prop 10 law does just that. At least the state is not willing to let poor kids die. The First 5 Commissioners, on the other hand, are fighting to do just that."

In my opinion, when the politicos **all** demonstrate behavior that any Joe might think is *void of character*, they really are ALL the <u>same</u> type of people, regardless of party affiliation.

IS THE LEFT NOW *THE NEW RIGHT*?

And so, it appears that these folks have no ethical problem with using the public's money to sue, after all, *it's for the children.*

Did you chomp at that? I didn't, and so why did I conclude that this heart-wrenching agency - who is good at promoting their efforts with cute pictures of smiling children - is of questionable value?

Because many newspapers have documented that First 5 Commission funds have repeatedly paid for Jelly Belly Factory tours, weekend trips for parents at expensive hotels, belly dancing classes and basic babysitting, amongst other non-impactful activities. When you compare that with the state wanting to use those funds to prevent childhood deaths, you just have to ask yourself: *is there character void in play here*?

My opinion: "*What's in it for me?*" gone amuck. Could that money be better used? I think that's an emphatic *yes* too. If the Left wants to challenge or reduce class differences, do they really have to create agencies with conflict of interest waivers and self-dealing to get there? Did they think the Right was going to show up and steal the money if they did not write in those provisions? *Really?*

It's well understood that conflict of interest laws are put in place to ensure that representatives on Boards like this one will not succumb to back room deals. In other words, conflict of interest laws exist so that people don't end up on the potentially illegal side of what happens when people act to resolve their cognitive dissonance in questionable or illegal ways.

If they come up on a vote to approve a budget that gives their own agencies most of the money, and as news reports show, *they do receive most of the money*, do you really think they are going to vote "*no*"? Heck no! They will rationalize away cognitive dissonance as "*My agency needs this money more than other ones in the community*".

I can only think that there must be some fierce competition to get a spot on one of those boards.

In line with some arguments put out there on the blogs, I think that law probably needs a serious revise so that people who serve on the Commissions can't receive <u>any</u> funding - OR - perhaps the law should be overturned.

Apparently some legislators have tried, but the knee-jerk reaction to photos of children playing happily on their new playground equipment seem to have been too heart-felt an image to overcome - at least so far . . . but things are changing in the American attitude towards questionable spending choices.

And I think, as a result of questions that arise from even minor reading of that law, that any Joe can probably assume that good things have not been happening there - and it turns out: they have not. Nine members of an advisory board for the San Diego First 5 Commission immediately quit when a rule was changed so that if they continued to serve on the advisory board, their agency could no longer receive funds (August 2009, from the San Diego Union Tribune website: SignOnSanDiego.com,).

Could that sound any more like the kind of behavior you would only expect on places like Wall Street"

Now just **who** is in it *only for the money?* Clearly, says this Joe, virtually all of them.

I'm wrapping up this example, but to learn more, look up First 5 Commission, Fullerton's Future Children and Family Commission Consultant gets $200 per hour to write on Facebook, and First 5 Grand Jury Finds Problems. Here's one I like: Orange County First 5 Executive Director receives over $300,000 in compensation - - and they say government workers are underpaid.

The final point of irony I leave you with is that it's almost a given that if the First 5 Commissions were paying for some kind of Right wing associated activity, say charter schools, the Left would be the first to argue that the conflict of interest issue had to be rectified - *immediately.*

Ahhhh, the smell of hypocrisy, legalized exemption to self-deal, and the stench of evidence showing that perhaps "*the Left is now the new Right*".

THE RIGHT'S EFFORTS

Is there anything more Right than the Tea Party Movement? Maybe not, let's find out.

Now I do not have as many data-driven points to make about them as I did about the First 5 Law, mainly because it's new and there are not many data points. And while we can't get into the minds of children to find out how the First 5 effort may impact their political views later on, the Tea Party

Movement gives us a unique opportunity to ask why people have been motivated to join.

While a lot are religiously oriented older white males, a surprisingly large minority are not. A lot of them are under 50 and reflect a lot of the demographics found in America at large ("*Tea Partiers Are Fairly Mainstream in Their Demographics*", April 5, 2010, Gallup website): **30% call themselves moderate or liberal** - and those are no small numbers.

A lot of what has been written about them has been somewhat conjecture as they have no central representative organization to establish their boundaries. I believe the Wikipedia entry and the Gallup polls are both good starting points should you wish a deeper look.

My own white parents did not have much education, and I am going to point out some stereotypes about the white and less educated to later make some larger serious points, so no thinking I am being an education-bigot or that I am using people for cannon fodder. The fact is that other people have made fun of these folks *too much* without asking some deeper questions about where their large motive force is coming from. I believe that answering such questions just might help folks understand each other and reach compromise to fix what ails America.

Here's a question: *Did you know that 28% of Americans polled in that same Gallup survey are in support of the Tea Party movement?*

On some level, as 68% of the Gallup responders did not report having a college degree, I believe some on the Right can probably be accused of convincing less than college educated and unemployed people that someone is "*taking something from them*" and that they should have a tea party to *get it back*. I believe this the primary inflammatory sloganizing ploy I have observed being used to manipulate emotions.

My question, as an attempt to break the jargon-hold: *was the middle upper class American Dream **ever** possible to be yours **or** was your belief that you too would partake at that level mainly due to the media marketing campaign of an optimal American lifestyle represented as being attainable by everyone?*

Ok, so the image of jeans wearing guys in pickup trucks with gun racks sitting down for a tea party is admittedly humorous for most of us to imagine. I keep trying to see if the stereotypic Bubba and company would lift their little pinkies up when sipping on that china, but that's just not working as an image I can hold in my mind - at least not without a bit of mirth.

But, keeping it real, what's not just a stereotype is that probably a lot those good old boys in the 1980s did not want to do more than get through high school, go for some technical school training, get themselves a cheerleader for a wife, and now, 10 to 20 years past the typical age of college, they are complaining that this country *done them wrong*. At least that's how people in the higher echelons of the

Left, most of whom have healthy incomes, seem to prefer to portray them.

There seems to be a slice of truth in the idea that they feel "done wrong", as I have read their Facebook comments and so forth, but it's not the whole of it by any measure. Just how did they get to believe that a high school education or just *some* college could get them to an middle upper class life? And are the surveys that suggest that the American schooling system is failing and is no longer competitive in the world epitomized in the lives of these people?

Well, whatever all the variables are that got us here, a success gap now exists; and even if you do not think it is your fault that there is a gap and you can look in the mirror and feel your decisions had nothing to do with it, that success gap is something we arguably have to more consciously address.

I believe it is a complicated set of interacting trends and decisions made economically and politically, individually and collectively. It's my view that cognitive dissonance and political polarizations are more easily rationalized, and so thrive in frustrated situations like that faced by this group and the millions of others like them, or at least in those who are somewhat like them in life circumstances.

In sum, I contend that the economic fallout from the last couple decades due to voids in character and bad behavior in many aspects of American life has disproportionately impacted those in the under 50 crowd who have found the Tea Party Movement attractive.

So, let's look closer.

There are community values somewhat unique to many small to medium towns across America, and well entrenched across the South and the Heartland in cities of all sizes. So, what factor other than long term unemployment helped the Right attract at least a good portion of the Tea Party membership?

My opinion: *through the virtual religious status afforded to high school football.*

Ok, when you are done laughing, here's what I mean.

Admittedly, I am using football symbolically to make a point, but there is also some grit to it. And people in the midlands and the southern states humorously refer to high school football as a quasi-religion themselves, so I am not covering new ground.

Their assignment of football to a quasi-religion I would contend means that people recognize that high school football is a huge part of a popular culture in which values have been set and goals have been achieved. My contention is that you could probably also argue it could be what influenced some of their young minds when they were figuring out what to do with their lives.

Compared with other segments of the country, a "live and let life happen" approach to life was adopted by a lot of the midland and southern people, perhaps somewhat influenced by the notion that "*God has a plan for each of us*". This somewhat prevalent attitude is probably is why not many on the Left took them as seriously as perhaps they could have were they to try to get them on board. Nonetheless, these are the core of folks many on the Left marginalize as *them dumb Texans* or Georgians or whatnot.

So, it's my Joe on the couch perspective that, in order to try to get two birds going with one stone: "*Obama and energizing "the football keg set*" - some Righty stealth marketing folk got together and realized there was a marketing opportunity, and they decided to help Keep It Simple: let's create something that sounds patriotic, let's be sure it's grassroots, heck, *let's have a tea party. It will keep things polarized, just the way we want them.*

Now the impetus may have been Rick Santelli's rant on CNBC about mortgages, but it quickly gained some steam, pushed on Fox TV and Glenn Beck, but **what's key** is that no centralized organization has taken root, they do <u>not</u> all vote Republican, and they are all <u>not</u> white males over 50.

So you can try to frame them as simply a Right wing campaign, and even though I contend that probably a good chunk of Right wing dollars were sent that way to keep them voting Republican (thus giving wing to the notion of "astroturfing" - versus "grassrooting"), I think you would be missing out on some telling and important information if we are ever to be able to move towards compromise.

When you look at who is a supporter, these football loving folks are no George W. Bush, and many have been traded down the employment ramp for the last 20+ years by politicians, corporations, and the media. They have been treated as expendable and unworthy of political or economic protection. They were in the vortex of "*the giant sucking sound*" that Ross Perot predicted. And when I talk about this group, I am not talking about the entrepreneurial segment of society who seems to be born with the genes and/or motivation to start and run successful businesses without finishing a college degree, which includes Bill Gates, for example, so let's keep that clear.

The group I am talking about is your average person who did not obtain a four year degree yet who thought the middle class American Dream was also within *their* grasp - because it was hammered into them as possible since they were tots and they were taught that their relative accomplishments as compared with the media model of the American Dream is how they should value their own worth.

Ok, so maybe it's not completely high school football's fault, though it was low hanging fruit to assign some blame, but I want to point out that high school football is symbolic of an emphasis on *short term thinking* and I contend it reflects how a lot of people were not taught to *delay gratification.*

My opinion: **the successful ability to delay gratification is how people move up the social strata** and that includes sacrificing immediate desires to finish bachelor degrees. (Post-bachelor is where the big bump in income occurs, as per Gallup and U.S. Census surveys.)

If you can't delay gratification, it's going to be hard to make that move upwards. You have to be able to save, not buy the 60" TV, the big truck tires, and so forth. But a focus on short term gratification, I think I can reasonably argue, is found in the principles of high school football. The message those kids get is that what is important in life is a football game: there are clear winners and losers and this game is winnable in 60 minutes - it just takes brawn, game preparation, and determination.

I believe a lot of them, *perhaps as a result of not being taught anything else*, carried a simple "*win or lose*" framework for assessing life into adulthood. The focus to be on the winning team has made them, and to be fair, millions of others with a similar point of view, vulnerable to those who emotionally manipulate through inflammatory sloganizing.

In other words, it is because they have developed a particular emotional vulnerability, in part through having been raised in communities that highly value a sport focused on short term strategies, that they have been vulnerable to being impacted by the Tea Party's "*win or lose*" and "*we can fix everything in 60 minutes*" message **if only** we win by kicking everyone else out. The politicians and the media know this, and if you did not, now so do you.

JUNIOR COLLEGE COHORT

Ok, Joe, you say, but there are a good number of people with college degrees in the Tea Party.

Maybe so, but I am focusing on the ones without a bachelor's degree for a particular reason: their impact on the future may be bigger than you think.

These average folks, and others around the country who fit a similar bill, comprise what I have come to call: the Junior College Cohort. Again, I am **not** making fun of them, enough people make a living out of it. I am just trying to apply an appropriate label so we can talk about the situation more easily.

The cohort comprises the type of folks that used to work in factories in this country; they filled that working class, somewhat educated spot in our economy, jobs that did not require a four year degree. And did you know - - as of 2009, according to the U.S. Census only about 35% of this country has a bachelor's degree or higher?

I believe the popular media fantasy is that everyone has a degree and that this is just some small group.

NO!

In the Gallup poll, 68% of the Tea Party members did not have a bachelor's degree. They are the majority; and, whether you like it or not: they are us, we are them, we are Americans together; they are part of **our** American community.

And now, they are getting lined up to vote for drastic change; and "they" literally shocked at least one NY seat out of the Left's hands recently, so they can't be ignored anymore, can they?

The jobs for a good chunk of these folks flat out got exported, and to tie it together from a prior example - those jobs essentially were sent to China's steel industry - as well as Taiwan's electronics industry and India's growing clothing industry.

While I am a big fan of "Protestant work ethic" - which assumes that the individual will be rewarded through their own hard work - the facts are that one simply cannot fulfill basic needs, let alone any higher rewards, if there is no work left here in America due to the exportation of jobs and the importation of high ticket goods that potentially undermine all of our industries here. It seems to me there's got to be more balance here; other countries insist on it, why shouldn't we?

Keeping it real: a high unemployment rate, should it be sustained for those with a short term view and a commitment to the ownership of guns, could create an unstable and perhaps violent and volatile society. If high unemployment persists for these groups, simply said, I believe it could make our country a very unsafe place to live. Unfortunately, there are extremists, some in the Tea Party, who are talking about *the next revolution*; it's my view that we should be paying more attention to their alienation.

So, as a result of the decision to import that bridge in San Francisco, I'd bet that some of the people who might have fabricated it instead might only able get across it on a bus since they may have had to sell their car should they have been on unemployment for a long time.

Now, I ask you, isn't that image of the worker *more* heart-wrenching than spending the Meathead Law money on children's belly dancing classes? It's easily arguable to me that it is **more** heart-wrenching to see an adult who cannot take care of themselves at age 40 than it is to feel guilty at all about the kid who is not getting more trips to the Jelly Belly factory.

And, as I said, I am a fan of international trade, but I do not think all of those jobs *had* to be exported, and here's my theory on the results of this job exportation trend:

What did many in the Junior College Cohort first do for work? A lot of them became the dot com sales force for phantom products - and that industry crashed.

What did many in the Junior College Cohort then do for work? A lot of them became the real estate sales force, joined the construction trade, or tried their hand at house flipping - and that industry crashed.

What is the cohort going to do next? Who knows? All I know is that we now have a lot of folks who are trained mainly as sales reps who need something to do and cannot find much of anything that is stable or upwardly mobile.

I believe this continued hammering has made them very pissed off because they were told that the American Dream was possibly theirs too; it seems clear to me that they are a big enough number to have a mobilizing impact on society in ways some people might not like. Maybe some will get into solar and other green business sales, but in the meantime, it's my theory that in part due to a least some of them being vulnerable to "quick solution" messages, they were easily influenced by the Right leaning message of the Tea Party movement: *"where's mine?"*.

The Right appealed to their disenfranchisement from the American Dream. Are they racist? Keeping it real, some probably are, but as there are a good number of people of color in the Tea Party, the traditional explanations just do not hold.

My opinion: **the Tea Party is driven by economics more than it is by politics.** They have reacted to the financial crisis more than to the underlying core belief system of the Right. In fact, the Gallup poll shows just that: they are not all Righties; but they all want change. Here you might argue that I have undermined my own argument about the Right emotionally manipulating these people.

No, what I am saying is that the Right did their part to manipulate and so generally the Tea Party is aligned with the Republican aisle. The *difference* with the Tea Party is that they are **not** responding to that manipulation by playing party politics the way it has always been done - and that is new.

And so whether or not you agree with their politics, they are in part doing what I am suggesting: they are not buying into traditional political messaging. They are causing problems in Washington with how they are trying to get things done, but at least they are for now, trying to avoid trading favors. The results remain to be seen.

IMPLICATIONS OF THE COHORT

Ok, so what motivated these people to take such a hard stance?

In my opinion: many of these folks are the people who went bankrupt. Their houses foreclosed. Their credit ratings plummeted and those low scores may be preventing them from getting a new job. They got burned as buyers because they were not taught basic finance in high school and cannot afford to *buy* a degree to elevate out of their situations; and they may not have the knowhow to delay gratification.

Their futures may be relatively bleak and they will likely <u>never</u> catch up in earnings to where people like them in the prior generation or where the baby boomers were at age 40. Because they have not and could not contribute much to Social Security since their wages were depressed or went up and down, the math says that they will be a huge drain in the future - on top of everything else we face.

The government's predictions about when Social Security empties *relies on the math assumption that people are working* - but what if this unemployment picture for the Junior College Cohort goes on for years? How soon could Social Security be bankrupt then? These are "Black Swan" questions, but who else should be asking them besides me, and if they are not, why not?

So, these cohort folks perhaps won't ever own a house or condo to live in and rentals might be their way through life. These people might live in bigger groups in smaller houses. These folks are not proud of themselves or their current station in life. Their confidence and self-esteem, as the Left claims *must* happen in these situations, have been damaged, probably irreparably. By now, when they interview for a job, they are likely showing the signs of long term stress in their bodies and even if most of them are not keg partying anymore, if they ever did, they look drained.

What's odd is that, in researching this book, I read a lot of Tea Party Movement blogs and Facebook comment sections and a lot of these folks are centrists at heart; the Gallup poll showed that **30% call themselves moderate or liberal**. It's clear to me that some are just seriously dissatisfied with the American Dream promises that were made to them. Any cognitive dissonance about joining the Right could easily have been offset with "*What has the Left done for me lately?*"

I think I can contend that at least 30-40% of the Tea Partiers who I've seen participate online might have been persuaded to the Left, but the Right jumped in and capitalized on the anger, disenfranchisement, and cognitive dissonance felt in such people.

What's ironic? This group is leveraging the Right into, believe it or not, a new level of diversification.

Yes, to me at least, in 2011, the Right became diversified along its spectrum, to wit Michelle Bachmann as compared with John Huntsman as compared with Herman Cain. It currently does not see *diversity* as positive thing in the same way that the Left does, and it seems as though it is afraid to even consider that the *diversified* definition could apply to them, after all, *diversity* is a *Lefty* slogan.

Confusion due to this new diversity and the presence of the Tea Party candidates was evident in the first Republican primary debate. No one really seemed to know how to deal with the Tea Party candidates, as in: "*Do we have to take this seriously? Do we have to give them the VP job?*" The question is how will they deal with their own changing face? WASPy conformity and getting everyone in line has been their modus operandi for decades. Now they have these *uppity* women, at least one African American, and some not so simplistic Right wing men like Ron Paul making their voices known loudly.

But should the Right "get it" and start talking it up about *their* diversification, they might snag the clue that by doing so explicitly, they could diffuse the power that phrase has on some centrist voters. Until then, this Joe plans to enjoy the humor watching them figure it out.

AND - - it should be interesting to see if they can "close the deal" to bring in the Junior College Cohort on a permanent basis. My opinion: it depends on whether they really have the under 50 Junior College Cohort by the emotional cajones or if it's just yet another phase of the Cohort looking for a stable emotional and economic place to call their own, since they now probably do not own much of anything.

* * * * * * *

In sum, it was not that hard to bring to you examples of how the parties may be actively manipulating behavior with basic marketing designed to force deeper political divisions and/or reinforce people's biases. Are they consciously manipulating to develop future voting blocks? I think so, and on both sides.

The First 5 Commission is probably doing so given its undocumented results while seeming to ensure one particular ethnic group receives most of the funding. I believe that the Tea Party is comprised a good deal from the Junior College Cohort, especially on the younger side, and that it was no accident that the centrists in that group were easily influenced to veer Right; the idea of government continuing to spend like crazy while so many of them are out of work has simply been untenable and so carried with it massive motive power. Who knows how many folks who showed up at the early meetings were sent there by the established Right to keep an eye on things and help steer the dialogue?

And no matter where the Tea Partiers land politically, they definitely are not happy with the government and its workings. They have been forcing the rest of us to pay attention to some of those things America ignored for a long time, including the specific costs of running the country. In doing so, they highlighted an ignored group who in fact has largely benefited from the lack of oversight: government workers.

Ahhh, yes, government workers: seen as leeches to the Right and class levelers to the Left, and as such, deserve some of our attention as we turn attention to ***the nation's economic problems***.

OUR ECONOMIC PROBLEMS

We're going to start here with government worker pensions. It's a fairly controversial topic and I find I have something kind of in depth to say about them.

So, when we talk pensions, let's skip the person who started their job at $30,000 and retired making $45,000 a year. Let's say they worked for 20 years or so with a 3% raise for four steps and maybe a cost of living adjustment every few years and whose pension would be somewhere in the range of $2,000-2,500 per month. Since most of those folks did not pay into Social Security, this is really nothing to argue over; that's almost trading pension dollars for Social Security dollars plus what they would have if they added to a 401(k) or a 403(b).

The problem is the top 20% who make $75,000+ and also are taking advantage of 457 and 401(a) plans while also getting a defined benefit pension. They are essentially "triple contributing" and when they take it out during retirement, they are "triple dipping". This fact has not surfaced well enough to get into the public's crosshairs, but this specific elitist activity is one of the main reasons I am writing this little tome.

The argument for pensions was that government employees were not getting enough salary to pay into their own retirement. In my opinion, that is simply not mathematically true if they also pay *anything* into a 457 deferred compensation plan and/or a 401(a). A 401(a) is a money purchase plan that is contributed to by either or both employee or employer, generally seen as an employee retention instrument. When you hear higher paid employees complaining, see if they have access to a 457 and / or a 401(a). The very presence of either of those investing options completely undermines the argument that "*we're not paid enough and we need defined benefit pensions with all the bells and whistles*".

Also, it's my contention that the unfunded portion of current government workers' pension obligations that will be due in the future (the "UAAL") is compensation that *should be negotiable* since the employee unions argue that it is "*compensation deferred*". Since they argue that it is "*salary I am not taking now and will get later*" then it is **salary**, <u>not</u> *benefit.* That means that this Joe thinks that unions should have to help pay those unfunded portions that will be due **current** employees in the future by deductions from those same **current** employee paychecks, i.e. increase their contributions.

NO ONE WAS WATCHING

And why do I think that higher deductions should come from current employees? Well in part, it's my opinion that the unions highly contributed to the problem by asking for too much and did not do their fiduciary duty to the public (and to their union members) to watch the eggs in the investment basket over the past decades. If current employees had to share in funding these pension deficits, do you think then that someone in the unions would actually *care* about how the pension funds are invested in the stock and housing markets? *Yep, I think so.*

The other main reason the pensions are in trouble has a lot to do with the poor investing of the pension funds; some in the field say that the investment managers are *a little too close* to the investment committee selecting them; to me this suggests that bribery should be looked into. It's my perspective that pension assets have been invested far too aggressively for assets that have so many fiduciary restrictions on them. No matter what, it's clear that those "*what would a prudent man do*?" restrictions should be better enforced.

I'd venture that 99% of the people in this country, if investing for their own child's education, would **never** invest the way the pension boards do, and yet few people understand just how risky the pension boards have been. Some of them had paper losses exceeding 70% during the last downturn. Some of them had exotic mortgage investments.

Some have invested directly in real estate buildings, for instance. Did you know that? Articles written on the topic contend that some plans will never recover without a major inflow of new dollars to *replace* permanently lost dollars and **that** is a major reason why the pension obligations have shot up so high.

So, <u>it takes a village to create a pension disaster</u> and it's not just the unions that you should be looking at here: it's the investing committee of the pension boards, generally made up of ex-firemen and other pensioners. These members are flown, by the way, all expenses paid by the pension boards (yes, by public dollar contributions), to exotic locales like Hawaii for week-long "investment training", complete with golf afternoons, of course. Some pension board members take 10 - 15 trips like this *per year*. You wouldn't think then that they would have lost a dime of public money in the investments, being so financially educated and all, now would you?

It would be nice if several pension issues were addressed at once, but how come it takes little old Joe to explain where the legal leverage is in this problem? I'm not a lawyer, but I know a legal contradiction when I see one: you simply cannot argue that a pension is deferred *salary* and then simultaneously claim it is a *benefit.* And if they are not following *the prudent man rule* for investment decisions, then why are they still on those boards?

Who will take them on? A recent Google search showed that the City of San Jose, California is going to try, but the State of California Attorney General called that "*ill advised*" - that coming from a future pensioner of course.

The Wisconsin Supreme Court, on June 14, 2011, overturned a lower court's ruling such that the state's workers collective bargaining rights are now capable of being altered so that they are able only to bargain for salaries, unless of course, new lawsuits filed against it prevail. If it stands, the change will allow the state to control benefit costs as just about any other employer is able to do when revenues are reduced.

A LOST INVESTMENT

And ... if the Wisconsin law stands, the state will potentially no longer have to layoff younger workers, who are in the process of learning the managerial ropes, because the state will have more money since it will probably not have to pay out as much in benefits. The investment in younger worker know-how can be saved if they are not forced to leave the sector; this used to be a valued process in this country.

The fact is a lot of governments and municipalities have 80%+ of their payroll at the highest salary levels for the position, and those folks have 20 - 25+ years of service, and thus, seniority rights. When seniority protected staff are allowed to stay on due to union contracts that leaves people in their 30s and 40s, who have reached a journeyman level of knowhow, at risk of losing their positions.

So when a journeyman with 10 years of experience and knowledge is laid off they take that knowhow into the private or nonprofit sector, and in such a situation, the government has potentially lost exceptional managerial talent come 7 - 15 years down the road.

As such, I feel that this is another inter-related issue the public taxpayers really need to get our heads around as we confront our future decisions; the seniority provisions of union contracts I feel should be re-negotiated - perhaps not fully given up - but re-negotiated so we do not lose *all* of the managers-in-development.

WHO CARES?

So I asked an attorney why there was no action from the legal community regarding government pensions, perhaps as a citizens' class action suit - just curious - and he told me the reason he would never sue the state over pensions is that the police are in unions and, then he seemingly joked, "*They have guns*". I pressed him on it and he proved to be serious. His view was that the safety unions had essentially blackmailed the municipalities into higher rates of pension. As in: "*You don't want criminals to break into your neighborhood, do you Mr. Mayor, hint, hint?*"

As stated elsewhere in some good news articles ("*Public Unions Take On Boss to Win Big Pensions*", NY Times 06/22/11), the fact that the government workers can vote in or out their bosses who negotiate their pay makes the situation unlike pensions in the private sector. The unions have ongoing influence over that official's labor negotiation proposals and they wield that power openly, removing those from office who do not play ball.

Because of this ability to manipulate the outcome, it seems to me that the pension situation in America begs for a third party intervention: us, the taxpayers and/or lawyers acting on behalf of us, the taxpayers, though I admit that perhaps public pressure on elected officials could be sufficient if strong.

No matter how it gets done, if the pension obligations and Other Post-Employment Benefits (called OPEB) for those currently working as government employees are not returned to the bargaining table as part of the negotiation, government as we know it will continually and increasingly be faced with shutting down services and/or closing for furlough periods. We could have government offices open on half time schedules, getting only half done of what they currently do.

GOVERNMENT RETIREE INTERIMS

One "easy" intervention to address a couple egregious issues in the pension and government worker arena would be to pass state and federal laws to prevent retired employees from coming back AT ALL and acting as interim replacements for the job they left or, for that matter, for any other public job.

In my opinion, it is *not enough* to pass a law so that they are prevented from taking pension while in those interim roles receiving salary, as some can receive even larger pensions after leaving the interim role if there is not ALSO a provision that they cannot receive further pension service credit for the time spent as an interim.

In other words, there are some jurisdictions where the interim gains additional pension after they leave the interim position, due to the increased number of months of service for having been an interim. When you add it all up, someone like that (and a Google search will show I am presenting it as it is in some locales) these retirees can be benefitting on a QUINTUPLE basis:

1) the interim salary

2) the additional service credit that increases their base pension pay after they leave the interim role

3) the pension that they may receive while also acting as an interim

4) the 457 deferred compensation plan income

5) the 401(a) money purchase plans

Yes, that's **FIVE** areas from which interim highly paid government retirees can take income or otherwise might be able to increase their total future income - at least at a higher level than I believe most people thought was even possible. Did you know that? Sound slightly elitist or like a backroom Wall Street deal? It does to me.

As a point of comparison, in the private sector, interims are obtained from outside or someone is temporarily promoted into the position. Most businesses know it is not a good idea to bring back the retiree as they want and need younger people to develop into the leaders of tomorrow.

Common sense dictates that it is important to develop future leadership and so it's my opinion that we should become more educated about it with the idea of eliminating these $200-300K+ incomes for interim government retirees.

BUT . . . the pension problem just points to bigger economic issues we face.

Yes, it's been done before. There are plenty of books that painfully go through each problem in dry academic volumes or produced by the government in 1,000 page budget documents.

However, it's possible to just detail them out simply so that people can take in the data easily and so I am going to do that here. You may have seen the headline, "*Taxpayers on the hook for $3 trillion in pensions*" (CNNMoney, August 19, 2010), but why I have bothered to write this book is that *it is not just $3 trillion that we face.*

Just imagine a rogue wave.

THE TOP 10 LIST

Rogue Wave: *an unexpected wave that is thought to be the result of the additive action of many smaller waves resulting in one wave of a height that exceeds* **"twice the significant wave height (SWH), which is itself defined as the mean of the largest third of waves in a wave record."** (Wikipedia)

I contend that it is *the additive situation* that is the problem; and that combined with denial and voids in character has created a rogue wave of issues. We have been avoiding dealing with it head on for at least a couple of decades. We get caught by the media or in the polarizing call of one party or another in blaming the problem of the day on the person of the day or the special interests, or what not.

It is our additive or aggregate apathy that let it get this far, but it can be our aggregate concern and a new commitment to American community that can bring about the changes needed.

You might react here and say: "*it's too complex, they all interact*". Yes, they do, and that's my point in terms of why it's important for us to get our minds around it now.

Because it is all complex, it is also why it's important to free our minds from the emotional manipulation of *whomever* with *whatever* motive they might have, and take a clear view towards seeking real dialogue and problem solving. Here's my Top Ten list:

- **Housing** - Not everywhere, but prices continue to drop such that the tax base will continue to drop which means lower revenues to government. The mortgage interest rate re-sets are expected to peak just this year, in mid-2011, (www.calculated riskblog.com/2007/10/imf-mortgage-reset-chart.html), and the market could teeter completely into collapse. What's potentially worse this time around is that these are interest rate re-sets for the higher priced mort-gage owners, like lawyers and doctors - the people who still have been buying all the consumer products.

  [Note that I said they are "*mortgage owners*", not *homeowners*. Why? Because homeowners actually own their homes outright. Point? "*Homeowner*" is another inflammatory gotcha phrase.]

- **Unemployment** - it is painful and frustrating for a lot of people, but what it also means is that high unemployment levels mean people buy less, so sales tax has dropped and shows no signs of significant pick up in the near or midterm future. The Junior College Cohort and the High School or less educated continue to have very high unemployment rates.

- **Debt** - America's total debt is about $55,000,000,000,000 as of late June, 2011 (www.usdebtclock.org). For fiscal year 2011, the interest that the country pays on the debt is calculated to be $275,335,099,277 (from Treasury Direct web site). Unless we pay off principal or take on less debt, this number will rise, and not just because of new bonds the government issues, but because the interest rates are expected to go up in the next few years.

- **Wages** - Wages are being pressured downward by international trade, and in construction and other historically strong tax producing industries, including steel fabrication.

  This has a rippling effect; for instance, in Seattle, it historically was calculated that one Boeing job was estimated to create 5 other jobs in the community

- **Public Pensions & Unions** - Budgets are being cut while government pension obligations are rising, in part again, due to unions forcing the government to keep on the most senior people. Unions were initially intended to protect workers from mistreatment, not guarantee government workers elite economic status.

- **Social Security** - The current estimate is that Social Security will be drained by 2037. There are not as many people in Generation X as in the Boomer cohort (who will be in their 80s in 2037). Right now, this means there will be more coming *out* of Social Security than going *in* - and that is what is starting to happen.

  In 2037 though, that's when that group of Junior College Cohorts who are currently mainly in the range of 35 - 45 will be starting into their 60s. What value producing skills will they have then? How are they going to feed themselves? They certainly cannot pay what's needed to maintain Social Security if their wages remain depressed and they have persisting high rates of un-employment.

- **Municipalities and their Muni Bonds** - The muni bond sector is at risk for increased defaults due to reduced revenue streams to cities and other municipalities that issue them, thus potentially affecting million of fixed income retirees. If the muni bonds default or cities go bankrupt, we may have an increasing number of homeless old people to take care of, sooner than you might think.

  Wealthy people also buy a lot of muni bonds and these bonds are the way sewer projects, water projects, airport projects and the like are cur-rently built. The investment money comes from the bonds and the project is built, and then interest and principal from revenues are used to pay the bonds. If revenues drop for airport travel, which is reliant on people having enough money to travel, then the airport district may not be able to pay the interest on the bonds and therefore would "default". The muni bond insurer fiasco on Wall Street also made this risk of default more possible across the board.

- **Federal Budget** - According to the federal government, 57% of the FY 2012 $4.3 trillion budget is mandated by law (Social Security, Medicare, military pensions, etc.). The rest is discretionary. Nearly half of the 43% in discretionary budget went to military spending. Almost 5% went to paying interest on the debt. According to a summary on About.com on the U.S. Budget, "*the two major Senior programs, Social Security and Medicare, went from 28% of the budget in FY 1988 to 34% of the budget in FY 2008. ... By FY 2021, the OMB* (Office of Management and Budget) *projects that these two programs will rise to 35% of total spending.*" **

- **Food** - Prices have been going up quite a lot recently. Partly it may because, as the Atlanta Journal-Constitution reported on June 3, 2011, farmers cannot find enough migrant workers to help pick the food on their fields due to new immigration laws that crack down on illegals. Hence, some of the food rots and that food which makes it to market goes up in price because buyers bid up the price in order to make sure their customers get some.

How hard is it really to create an agreement that solves this problem? I contend it really is not as hard as some people make it out to be, but it may not be "*what's in it for me*" for enough people.

Also, fortunately for those on unemployment, there is no tax on the foods that are good for you. One idea is to tax junk food and not let people on food stamps buy crappy food - people have argued against that as a personal privacy issue, but really folks, it is taxpayer money. I personally am not much into social engineering but it is one of the few that makes some sense. Good food in, maybe better productivity and health out.

But beyond that, I'm no Michael Moore, but to become more educated about food in America, you might consider getting hold of a DVD called *Food, Inc.* How we get our food in America is something that maybe political parties, the government, or the food connected corporations do not want you to know, but I encourage you to find out more about *everything* that is going on, and this film calls out some data worth a review. If nothing else, it will make you want us to spend more on meat inspection.

- **Energy and Gasoline** - Ok, no lecture about global warming, but the facts are that there are limited resources for oil and other natural resources. As resources go down, prices go up. Efforts to go to electric cars capable of being recharged by solar seem to be something we can do rather quickly; same with home heating. As we look to ways to solve problems, here's a question: Did you know that the largest users of energy are retail and office buildings? Perhaps buildings built at least partially underground would help out. And besides, airplane terrorists can't drop a multiple story building if it's mostly submerged.

The main point I am trying to make here is that ***none of these issues exists as a problem without the presence of at least one of the other problems and*** *that they __all__ belong in an American dialogue at the same time.*

And yes, I know it's cliché to do a Top Ten, but . . .

Hey you! Wake up!   Well, if you are anything like I used to be, this is about where you would put this book down and go turn on the TV so you don't have to think about it anymore, at least for a while - but that's what they got people to do for about 50 years: turn on the boob tube.

Ahhh sedation! Or maybe a nap sounds good... but, you are in luck, this is where we will wind it down and figure out what we might do about this mess.

** *You may have noticed that I did not include health care in a separate bullet point. This is because I believe it belongs more saliently in a book about work life, but since it is a huge issue, it owns a chapter in my next book America's Real Deficit: Is Character Disorder Everywhere?*

SO NOW WHAT?

We have no choice but to deal with the Top Ten list. We simply have to take on these issues as we will be living in the country that we helped create. So the answer I probably have to you saying to me "*what's in it for me?*" might be me asking you back "*What's **not** in it for you?*"

It's just probably not an option anymore to block these issues out and rationalize it as someone else's problem. For some of you, and I don't intend to sound mean, but one suggestion I can offer is that perhaps you should get your nose perpetually out of your iPhone and take some time to think about your own role in the situation. (I think they could have called it the "*what's in it for mePhone*" but that probably would have been too obvious.)

So, how do <u>we</u> fix America's polarized government?

My opinion:

- First, you start by figuring out when someone in a political party or in the politicized media is hitting you with inflammatory jargonizing slogans.

- Second, you learn how to process it as jargon and figure out what part of it is real for you, if any.

- Third, you persist in seeking solutions after making sure everyone at the table knows you will not succumb into projective polarizations that prevent the group or the country from solving whatever problem it is.

- Fourth, you can solve more problems because you have enough people in alignment who understand that they will have to give a little, even sometimes a good bit, and occasionally even a lot.

This opinion is directed to you as the voter, the involved community member, the elected council member, the American legislatures, and all the way on up to the President.

Sure, the media and parties may be appealing to what's already in your heart, but when the media or politicos push your buttons with slogans, and you respond emotionally or take action to strengthen your commitment to the party line, it's my opinion that you could actually be helping them keep everything polarized, divisive, and party-political.

And so, to do my little part, I am going to ask you to try something:

When you are feeling conflicted about a political issue, become aware that cognitive dissonance may be in play. It's of course fine to just say to yourself: "*I am feeling conflicted about that and I don't have a clue what the answer should be as of today.*" I contend that such an answer is totally legit, but I also think you have to keep seeking information to eventually come to a position that works for you.

Then, the harder suggestion: perhaps take a hard look at the man or woman in the mirror.

What is it about you that tend towards voids in character? What *little bit of bad* is a weak spot in your armor such that the media and the politicos might be able to get you to take a side and dang it if you are not going to stay there till hell freezes over?

I am not saying become paranoid, but I am strongly suggesting that we pay attention and learn to make a productive distinction between political banter and what it takes to solve our issues. Perhaps look for where the parties could meet on an issue instead of joining in your party's knee-jerk blaming of special interests, the Right, the Left, the government, the wealthy, the poor, the corporations, or the last generation.

I simply believe that we have to make a mental shift away from letting the media and the parties keep us polarized, but I also suspect that change *will only take root* if change starts with each individual.

So it is a matter of personal choice, personal ethics, and personal character. If you find a reason to change as a result of doing this personal examination, perhaps those around you will be willing to do so as well.

I think it is our only real chance to make substantive change.

FOR EXTRA CREDIT

If it has not been clear, I am a centrist, and I want to give you a concrete example of how I confronted sound bites and got automatic agreement to shut off.

Perhaps my doing so may seem a little preachy or condescending to some of you, but honestly, I do not think it is a bad thing to hear how someone else broke down a problem to come to a conclusion; we all can get stuck in our analysis methods at one time or another.

So, here's my starting point: I used to believe that government pensions made some reasonable sense, even for highly compensated staff. I rationalized the deservedness of the pension, telling myself that we needed to pay them so that people would stay in government: the *"inability to attract talent without them"* argument.

I began to challenge the message that it would be a *"crime against middle class jobs"* if they were taken away, as my friends who lean Left would argue to me. What I confronted is that if you buy into that polarizing idea, it requires you to somehow concur that the main way class differences can be mitigated is to create government jobs with defined benefit pensions.

I grew tired of thinking that because it just did not explain enough about what was going on around me. Due to feeling that the argument was being dis-ingenuously applied by Left leaning folks, I began to feel I was just being manipulated by slogans, probably so that I did not ask some obvious *reality based* questions. When I did, here's what I came up with:

- Are defined benefit pensions the only way possible to improve the lives of people?

- Is it even possible to erase class differences?

- Can we even think that we will erase further class differences if we know the future will include both internationalizing forces influencing American wages and competition for natural resources such that the standard of living in America is likely to drop from what we know it to be now?

- What is the point of trying to erase the circumstances of a person's life if the public resources required to do that highly outweigh the benefit to society? And what if, when people "*make it*", their attitude becomes yet another illustration of void of character (i.e. they bail on paying taxes, pay household help under the table, etc.)?

- Is the choice really between keeping full pension government jobs as some emblem of doing something towards class parity OR must we get lean and force current employees to take cuts so their grandkids do not suffer so heavily? Or is it a choice between some other options entirely?

So, as many will no doubt have concluded already, in part I am asking you to do some Critical Thinking 101 exercises about what you think you believe.

I think we have to do far more basic critical thinking like this because the hard estimates indicate that the future is going to be ugly, at least for a while, during however long it takes us to right the ship. We are going to probably have to be willing to take some personal hits to get to a stable future and being lazy intellectuals won't get us anywhere.

Now, my cognitive dissonance kicks in here and sometimes my first reaction to these issues is much like many people: *it's not going to be **my** problem if only I am rich enough.*

My self-preservation urge is to go find some higher paying job and ignore every bit of bad behavior I see and to take the possible career hit on *not being caring enough* rather than being blamed for bringing up any ugly and/or illegal stuff. In other words, to let the ugly stuff continue unabated if necessary and be a bystander who gets paid well to keep my mouth shut. That approach pays off for highly educated liberals and conservatives alike. Why not me too?

However, my long term thinking and my inter-personal attitude kicks in and asks for a larger perspective on life, a commitment to character, and to my responsibilities as a citizen here in the USA.

A lot of people fought and died for my freedoms; I simply can't ignore those sacrifices.

But to sum it up for now, the middle-upper class American Dream as it has been portrayed, and even glamorized, in my opinion, is in part a marketing pitch that perhaps could not ever achieve its claims, at least not for all of us, maybe not even for most of us.

Instead, in attempting to reach the media inspired optimal level of the American Dream, people have become complacent in accepting apathy, voids in character and "*what's in it for me*" as attitudes and behaviors that are socially or politically justifiable to obtain a larger personal footprint at the expense of others, by playing dirty or altering the playing field in their favor.

I hope I have convinced you that allowing ourselves to be tied to one political side or the other is ***just not working*** for America anymore.

And I hope I've convinced you to consider that the responsibility to change is not somewhere ***out there***.

The problems started with us.

The solutions must also start with us.

ABOUT THE AUTHOR

Joe Couch, MBA, is a former CEO and business owner. He took the risks and received many of the rewards of attending a top-ranked Ivy.

And like many others, Joe was thrown into an sea of unethical behavior and asked to look the other way. But Joe thinks that approach to life got America into a serious jam and that it is high time we had a more complete dialogue about America and its future.

Joe isn't much of a complainer, but as more and more people talked to him about their lives, they told stories of work and play that were beyond belief.

It was then that it sunk in:

America really is messed up.

Joe badly wants this situation to change, and he has a few ideas to share about how we can do that . . . if we really want to.

A TEASE:

IS CHARACTER DISORDER EVERYWHERE?

Having finished this walk through the government-media sectors, I believe there are other areas of life where both character void and people not playing inside the lines is getting this country into some serious contradictions, now often resulting in improper legal actions in work life.

And because I feel we need to take these work life character issues out of the dark closet that they lurk in and shine the light dead center upon them, I'm starting a new conversation: "*America's Real Deficit: Is Character Disorder Everywhere?*".

So here's the book's teaser: there's a fictionalized story coming *from a workplace near you.* I don't think you'll find it boring. You might even see a dramatized portrayal of someone's boss that cuts a different slice through his or her motives - and - you might even be able to figure out some of the hidden reasons why people may be behave the way they do.

Ahhh, employment law, healthcare, executive pay, philanthropy, and "the leadership deficit" in Not-For-Profits . . . such a lovely set of incubators for cognitive dissonance and void of character challenges.